Praise for Reshma Saujani

'Reshma Saujani is . . . empowering "an army of young women" to take on tech's gender gap'
CNN

'I love this book! A timely message for girls and women of all ages: perfection isn't just impossible but, worse, insidious. The prose is so clear, so honest – you feel like you're sitting across from Reshma sharing stories.'
Angela Duckworth, *New York Times* bestselling author of *Grit*

'The perfect is not just the enemy of the good; the pressure to be perfect is the enemy of girls around the world. In this courageous, convincing book, Reshma Saujani shares a bold vision to free girls – and women – from the shackles of social expectations.'
Adam Grant, *New York Times* bestselling author of *Originals, Give and Take* and *Option B* with Sheryl Sandberg

'For any woman who has ever thought to herself "I just can't . . ." or "I'm just not . . .," this eye-opening book will help you showing up every day as brave, not perfect changes how the world sees you, but more importantly, how you see yourself - and what you are capable of. This book is great reminder that having the courage to stare your mistakes and your imperfections in the face is one of the most overlooked sources of power.'
Amy Cuddy, Harvard lecturer and Bestselling author of *Presence*

Reshma Saujani is the Founder and CEO of Girls Who Code, a national nonprofit organization working to close the gender gap in technology while teaching girls confidence and bravery through coding. A lifelong activist, Reshma was the first Indian American woman to run for U.S. Congress. She's been named a Fortune 40 under 40, a WSJ Magazine Innovator of the Year, and one of the Most Powerful Women Changing the World by *Forbes*. She is the author of three books, including *Women Who Don't Wait In Line* and the *New York Times* bestseller *Girls Who Code: Learn to Code and Change the World*. Reshma lives in New York City with her husband, Nihal, their son, Shaan, and their bulldog, Stanley.

Brave, Not Perfect

Fear Less, Fail More, and Live Bolder

Reshma Saujani

ONE PLACE. MANY STORIES

HQ
An imprint of HarperCollins*Publishers* Ltd
1 London Bridge Street
London SE1 9GF

This edition 2019

1
First published in Great Britain by
HQ, an imprint of HarperCollins*Publishers* Ltd 2019

A catalogue record for this book is
available from the British Library.

ISBN: HB: 978-0-00-824952-6
TPB: 978-0-00-824953-3

Printed and bound in Great Britain by
CPI Group (UK) Ltd, Croydon CR0 4YY

MIX
Paper from
responsible sources
FSC
www.fsc.org
FSC™ C007454

This book is produced from independently certified FSC™ paper
to ensure responsible forest management.

For more information visit: www.harpercollins.co.uk/green

To every "perfect" girl and woman:
You are braver than you know.

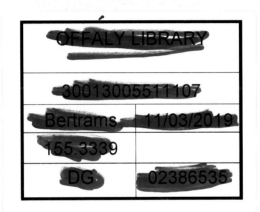

Contents

Daring the Unthinkable

In 2010, I did the unthinkable. At the age of thirty-three, never having held an elected position, I ran for US Congress.

Up until then, even though it had been my dream from the time I was thirteen years old to run for public office and effect real change, I had stayed safely tucked behind the scenes of politics. By day, I worked long, grueling hours in a big-name investment firm—a high-paying, glamorous job that I hated but stayed in because it was what I thought I was supposed to be doing. At night and in every spare moment on weekends, I worked as a fund-raiser and organizer; these were all valuable contributions that had impact, but in my heart, I wanted to play big and do big things.

With every passing day, I became more and more miserable in my job, until I reached a moment of deep despair when I knew something needed to change. That was when I heard a whisper in the New York political community that the sitting congresswoman in my district was going to vacate her seat after eighteen years to run for Senate. I knew this was my opening. I met with a few key people to ask what they thought, and everyone said enthusiastically that I should go for it. I knew how to raise money, I had good policy ideas, I had a good background story; although I had no experience personally running for office, the rest was there. For the first time in as long as I could remember, I felt fired up. I was finally heading toward the life of public service I'd always dreamed about, and there was no stopping me.

Then it happened. The congresswoman decided not to vacate her seat, which meant I would need to run against her if I wanted it. Suddenly, all the people who'd supported me and said go for it were saying, "Oh, no, no . . . you can't run against her." She was a venerable insider, a force to be reckoned with, and they said I didn't stand a chance. Not only did I lose the enthusiastic support of the female party elite—they outright told me it wasn't my turn and demanded that I back down.

But by that point, I was in too deep to give up. Here was my dream, just inches within reach. I *wanted* this—way too much to turn and run away. Believe me, there were plenty of moments that I thought to myself, *I must be nuts.* But I went for it anyway. I knew this would be my one shot and that I'd regret it for the rest of my life if I didn't take it.

To my surprise—and the surprise of a lot of other people—my race caught a lot of positive attention. Here I was, a young South Asian upstart who had never held public office, but people were listening, the campaign donations were flowing in; I was even endorsed by the *New York Observer* and the *Daily News.* I went from tentatively hopeful to confident I would win after being featured on the cover of two national newspapers, and having CNBC tout my race as one of the hottest in the country.

But when push came to shove, it turned out that voters cared a lot more about my lack of experience than anyone thought. I didn't just lose; I got clobbered, winning just 19 percent of the vote to my opponent's 81.

What's remarkable about this story isn't that I ran for Congress. Or how stunningly and spectacularly I ended up losing, or even how I picked myself back up after such a public and humiliating defeat. What makes this story worth telling is the fact that when I ran for public office at the age of thirty-three, it was the first time in my entire adult life that I had done something truly brave.

If you looked at my pedigree up until that point—Yale Law School, followed by a string of prestigious jobs in the corporate world—you probably would think I was a gutsy go-getter. But being a go-getter and being gutsy aren't necessarily the same. It was the drive to cultivate the perfect résumé that got me into Yale Law School after being rejected by them a whopping three times, not bravery. It wasn't genuine passion for the law or big business that compelled me to go after a job at a top-five law firm and then a premier financial assets management firm; it was the desire to please my immigrant father and fulfill his dreams for me. From the time I was a little girl, I had always set my sights on being the best, and every move I made was an effort to make me appear smart and competent and in turn open doors to other positions that would make me appear smart and competent. I made all these choices to build the "perfect me," because I believed that would lead to the perfect life.

Despite how things looked from the outside, none of my life choices up until that point were truly brave for one simple reason: there was nothing on the line. This was the first time I was going off-script, doing something that truly mattered to me, in a deeply personal way. It was the first time I had gone for something even though I wasn't 100 percent confident I could succeed and stood to lose far more than just the election if I failed. I could lose my dignity, my reputation, and my self-confidence. It could hurt, big-time. Could I recover from that?

I'm not alone in having spent my adult life only pursuing positions or projects I knew I'd ace. So many women stick to doing only the things at which they excel, rarely going beyond what makes them feel confident and comfortable. I hear this over and over from the thousands of women I meet around the country, regardless of their race, age, or economic circumstances. I heard it from the twenty-four-year-old dog walker I chatted with at Starbucks who had a fantastic idea for revolutionizing her service but was convinced she could never do it because she's "bad at business," and from the fifty-eight-year-old magazine editor I sat next to at a political fundraiser who told me she is miles past burned out and unhappy but won't leave her job, even though she can financially afford to. Why? Because, she says with a shrug, "It's what I'm good at." As CEO of the nonprofit Girls Who Code I see it in my young female employees who don't volunteer for projects in areas where they don't have prior experience, while the men jump hard and fast into unfamiliar territory without worrying one iota about failing or looking foolish.

There's a reason why we women feel and act this way. It has nothing to do with biology and everything to do with how we've been trained. As girls, we're taught from a very young age to play it safe. To strive to get all A's to please our parents and teachers. To be careful not to climb too high on the jungle gym so we don't fall and get hurt. To sit quietly and obediently, to look pretty, to be agreeable so we will be liked. Well-meaning parents and teachers guide us toward activities we excel at so we can shine, and they steer us away from the ones we aren't naturally good at to spare our feelings and grade point averages. Of course the intentions are good; no parent wants to see their daughter injured, disappointed, or discouraged. The bubble wrap in which we are cocooned comes with love and caring, so no one realizes how much it insulates us from taking risks and going after our dreams later in life.

Boys, on the other hand, absorb a very different message. They are taught to explore, play rough, swing high, climb to the top of the monkey bars—and fall down trying. They are encouraged to try new things, tinker with gadgets and tools, and get right back in the game if they take a hit. From a young age, boys are groomed to be adventurous. Research proves they are given freer rein to play on their own and are encouraged to attempt more daring physical activities with fewer directives and assistance from parents. By the time boys are teenagers asking someone on a date, or young adults negotiating their first raise, they are already well habituated to take risk after risk and are, for the most part, unfazed by failure. Unlike girls, they are rewarded with approval and praise for taking chances, even if things don't work out.

In other words, boys are taught to be *brave*, while girls are taught to be *perfect*.

Rewarded for perfection from the time we're young, we grow up to be women who are terrified to fail. We don't take risks in our personal and professional lives because we fear that we'll be judged, embarrassed, discredited, ostracized, or fired if we get it wrong. We hold ourselves back, consciously or unconsciously, from trying anything that we're not certain we'll ace to avoid the potential pain and humiliation. We won't take on any role or endeavor unless we are certain we can meet or exceed expectations.

Men, on the other hand, will jump into uncharted waters without hesitation or apprehension about what might happen if they don't succeed. Case in point: the now-famous corporate report that found that men apply for a job when they meet only 60 percent of the qualifications, but women apply only if they meet 100 percent of the qualifications.

We want to be perfect before we even try.

The need to be perfect holds us back in so many ways. We don't speak up for ourselves, as we know deep down we should, because we don't want to be seen as pushy, bitchy, or just straight-up unlikable. When we do speak up, we agonize and overthink how to express ourselves, trying to hit just the right note of assertiveness without seeming too "bossy" or aggressive. We obsessively analyze, consider, discuss, and weigh every angle before making a decision, no matter how small. And if we do, heaven forbid, make a mistake, we feel as though our world is falling apart.

And yet, when we hold ourselves back for fear of not being good enough, or fear of being rejected, we tamp down our dreams and narrow our world—along with our opportunities for happiness. How many offers or experiences have we passed up because we were afraid? How many brilliant ideas have we let go by, or personal goals have we backed away from, because we feared we wouldn't get it right? How many times have we begged off a position of leadership saying, "I'm just not good at that"? I believe this "perfect or bust" mentality is a big part of why women are underrepresented in C-suites, in boardrooms, in Congress, and pretty much everywhere you look.

This drive to be perfect takes a serious toll on our well-being, too, as we lose sleep ruminating over the slightest mistake or worrying that someone was offended by something we said or did. Trained to be helpful and accommodating at all costs, we run ourselves ragged trying to do it all and end up exhausted, depleted, even sick because we give away so much of our energy and time to others.

Our self-esteem takes a hit when we stay silent in moments we know we should have spoken up, or when we say yes when we really wanted to say no out of fear of not being liked. Our relationships and hearts suffer when we put up a glossy veneer of perfection; the protective layer may keep others from seeing our flaws and vulnerabilities, but it also isolates us from those we love and keeps us from forging truly meaningful and authentic connections.

Imagine if you lived without the fear of failure, without the fear of not measuring up. If you no longer felt the need to stifle your thoughts and swallow what you really want to say in order to please and appease others. If you could stop berating yourself mercilessly for human mistakes, let go of the guilt and the strangling pressure to be perfect, and just *breathe*. What if, in every decision you faced, you made the brave choice or took the bolder path. Would you be happier? Would you impact the world in the ways you dream you can? I believe the answer to both is yes.

I wrote *Brave, Not Perfect* because that pursuit of perfection caused me to hold myself back for too many years. At the age of thirty-three, I finally learned how to be brave in my professional life, which taught me how to be brave in my personal life, too. I've been exercising that bravery muscle every day since. It wasn't easy to go for in vitro fertilization after three devastating miscarriages, or to launch a tech start-up without knowing anything about coding (or about start-ups). But because I did these things, I am a deliriously happy mom to a little boy and am making a difference in the world in the way I always knew deep down I could.

When we relinquish the punishing need for perfection—or, rather, let go of the fear of *not* being perfect—we find freedom, joy, and all the other good stuff we want in life. It's time to stop giving up before we try. Because when we do give up on anything that is challenging or doesn't come to us naturally, we become trapped in a state of discontent and iner- tia that's soul crushing. We stay in the relationship that brings us pain, in the social circle that brings us down, in the career that makes us miserable. We let our good ideas wither and die on the vine; or, worse, we painfully watch others succeed at something we *knew* we should have pursued. Being afraid to try something new, to boldly ask for what we want, to make mistakes, and, yes, maybe even to look a little foolish leads to a lot of wasted brilliance, swallowed ambitions, and regret.

When we hold ourselves to the impossible standard of perfection, there's no such thing, really, as "success," because nothing is ever enough.

What if we just said, *Fuck it? I'm going to say what's on my mind even if they don't like it . . . or volunteer for that assignment that feels too hard . . . or make the life change I secretly dream about without worrying about the outcome.* What would our lives look like?

Letting go of the fear of being less than perfect is easier than you think. It all comes down to exercising your brav- ery muscles, one little bit at a time. That's what this book is about. It's a look at how we were wired way back when to pursue perfection and avoid failure at all costs, and how that girlhood wiring holds sway over us in our adult lives. Most importantly, it's about how to reset that wiring. It's never too late. By letting go of the need to be perfect and retraining ourselves to be brave, every one of us can dare her own ver- sion of the unthinkable.

Why Me?

How did I go from being a failed congressional candidate to a champion for women and bravery? Great question.

After I picked myself up off the floor—literally—in the weeks following my crushing defeat, I looked around and thought, *What's next?* As I searched inside myself for an answer, I thought about how, back when I was crisscrossing the city during my political campaign, I had visited numerous schools where I saw coding and robotics classes filled with boys, and how I couldn't stop thinking about the faces *I hadn't* seen. Where were the girls? It started to become clear to me that someone needed to take steps toward closing the gender gap in technology by reaching girls at an early age. Pretty quickly I knew that this was my next calling and how I would be of service in the big way I'd dreamed. By 2012, I'd founded Girls Who Code, which has grown into a national movement with more than ninety thousand girls in fifty states participating.

The original mission of Girls Who Code was to reverse the trend of girls' interest in STEM dropping off between the ages of thirteen and seventeen, so that by the year 2020, women will be on track to fill much more than just their current 3 percent of the 1.4 million jobs that will be available in computing-related fields. But once GWC got off the ground, I quickly realized we were doing far more than setting up these girls for future job success. By teaching them to code, we were also teaching them to be brave.

You see, coding is an endless process of trial and error with sometimes just a semicolon making all the difference between success and failure. Code breaks and falls apart, and it often takes many, many tries before you experience that magical moment when what you're trying to create comes to life. To get there requires perseverance and comfort with imperfection.

In February of 2016, I gave a TED talk based on what I'd

observed firsthand about girls, perfection, and bravery. The talk was a rallying cry to change how we were socializing our girls—and to encourage women to let go of our people-pleasing, perfectionist instincts and reclaim our voices, courage, and power.

The talk hit a deep nerve that took me by surprise. I knew the topic was profoundly meaningful to me, but it turns out that it resonated with thousands of girls and women around the country as well. Within days, emails started flooding in. Some women shared how they recognized themselves in the message. "I've been crying since I heard your talk," one wrote. "I realized how much I do this to myself," said another. I heard from countless women who shared how they had passed up opportunities because they were afraid of appearing foolish, of failing, of not living up to the impossible standards they set for themselves.

Some of the emails made me cry as I read how women and girls felt tyrannized by perfectionism: "When I make a mistake or let someone down, I beat myself up for days," one woman said. "It's all I can think about." Another wrote, "Everyone thinks I'm this person who has everything under control . . . if they only knew how hard I work to look that way and how afraid I am that someone will see the mess that I really am."

Others made me indescribably proud. One college sophomore wrote about how, after many years crying in frustration over homework, unable to ask for help, afraid of being seen as dumb, alienated in school because of her own fixation on perfection, she finally let go of her need to be perfect. "It was incredibly empowering," she wrote. "I can ask questions. So what if an ignorant person thinks I'm dumb because I need something clarified? I'm here for myself and my education."

I heard from parents of kindergartners worried about how

hyperconcerned their five-year-old girls were with doing everything exactly "right," and from educators who wanted me to know they had sent mass emails or newsletters to parents imploring them to watch my talk with their family.

The message of "brave, not perfect" continued to spread through bloggers and social media, and through interviews with major news outlets. As of the writing of this book, the TED talk has been viewed almost four million times. I've had the privilege of speaking at the Fortune Most Powerful Women Summit and with former first lady Michelle Obama at the United States of Women Summit in Washington, D.C.

That's all been exciting and gratifying, but for me, the most amazing part has been seeing firsthand how the "brave, not perfect" message is sparking personal and meaningful change. Each week, I travel to at least one or two cities to speak at conferences, schools, and corporations; and everywhere I go, I am overwhelmed and touched to learn how my talk inspired women and girls to try something new or intimidating, even if it scared the hell out of them. To ask the questions, or venture the answer, even if they worried they would look foolish or appear less than polished. To leave the "safe" career path for the one they'd always dreamed of, even if people told them they were crazy. To take that leap into the unknown, even if they knew they might stumble and fall—and trust that the world wouldn't come to an end even if they did.

I wrote this book because I believe that every single one of us can learn to be brave enough to achieve our greatest dreams. Whether that dream is to be a multimillionaire, to climb Mt. Everest, or just to live without the fear of judgment hanging over our heads all the time, it all starts to become possible when we override our perfect-girl programming and retrain ourselves to be brave.

No more silencing or holding ourselves back, or teaching

our daughters to do the same. It's time to stop this paradigm in its tracks. And just in case you're thinking that bravery is a luxury reserved for the 1 percent, let me assure you: I've spoken to women across a wide range of backgrounds and economic circumstances, and this is a problem that affects us all. My goal is to create a far-reaching movement of women that will inspire *all* women to embrace imperfection, so they can build a better life and a better world. No more letting opportunities go by, no more dimming our brilliance, no more deferring our dreams. It's time to stop pursuing perfection and start chasing bravery instead.

Anaïs Nin wrote, "Life shrinks or expands in proportion to one's courage." If this is true—and I believe that it is—then courage is the key to living the biggest life we can create for ourselves. I am writing this book because I believe every woman deserves a shot at breaking free from the perfection-or-bust chokehold and living the joyful, audacious life she was meant to lead.

Part One

How Girls Are Trained for Perfection

1

Sugar and Spice and Everything Nice

Sixteen-year-old Erica is a shining star. The daughter of two prominent professors, she is the vice president of her class with an impeccable grade point average. Her report card is peppered with praise from her teachers about her diligence and what a joy she is to have in class. She volunteers twice a month at a local hospital. At the end of sophomore year, she was voted "Best Smile" by her classmates, and her friends will tell you she's the sweetest person they know.

Beneath that bright smile, though, things aren't quite as sunny. If you open Erica's journal, you'll read about how she feels like it's her full-time job to be perfect in order to make everyone else happy. You'll learn that she works to the point of exhaustion every night and all weekend to get all A's and please her parents and teachers; disappointing them is just about the worst thing she can imagine. Once, because of an accidental scheduling mistake, she had to back out of a debate competition at school because it conflicted with a volunteer trip she'd committed to go on with her church; she was so hysterical that her teacher was going to "hate her" that she literally made herself sick.

Erica despises volunteering at the hospital (don't even get her started on emptying the bedpans . . .) but sticks with it because her guidance counselor said it would look good on her college applications. Even though she desperately wanted to try out for cheerleading team because she thought it looked like fun, she didn't, because her friends told her the jumps were really hard to learn and the last thing she wanted to do was make an idiot of herself. Truth be told, she doesn't really even like most of her friends, who can be mean and catty, but she just quietly goes along with what they say and do because it's too scary to imagine doing otherwise.

Like so many girls, Erica is hardwired to please everyone, play it safe, and avoid any hint of failure at all costs.

I know this story because today, Erica is forty-two and a good friend of mine. She is still supersweet with a dazzling smile—and still a prisoner of her own perfectionism. A successful political consultant with no kids, she works until after midnight most nights to impress her colleagues and overdeliver for her clients. Every time I see her she looks fabulously put together; she's that friend who always says just the right thing, always sends just the right gift or note, and is always on time. But just like her sixteen-year-old self, she'll only reveal privately that she still feels strangled by the constant need to please everyone. I asked her recently what she would do if she didn't care what anyone else thought. She immediately ticked off a list of goals and dreams she wished she had the guts to go after but wouldn't dare, ranging from telling her biggest client that she disagrees with his strategies to moving out of the city and having a child on her own.

Our culture has shaped generations of perfect girls like Erica who grow up to be women afraid to take a chance. Afraid of speaking their minds, of making bold choices, of owning and celebrating their achievements, and of living the life *they* want to live, without constantly seeking outside approval. In other words: afraid of being brave.

From the time they are babies, girls absorb hundreds of micromessages each day telling them that they should be nice, polite, and polished. Adoring parents and caretakers dress them impeccably in color-coordinated outfits (with matching bows) and tell them how pretty they look. They are praised mightily for being A students and for being helpful, polite, and accommodating and are chided (however lovingly) for being messy, assertive, or loud.

Well-meaning parents and educators guide girls toward activities and endeavors they are good at so they can shine, and steer them away from ones they might find frustrating, or worse, at which they could fail. It's understandable because we see girls as vulnerable and fragile, we instinctively want to protect them from harm and judgment.

Our boys, on the other hand, are given freedom to roam, explore, get dirty, fall down, and yes, fail—all in the name of teaching them to "man up" as early as possible. Even now, for all our social progress, people get a little uncomfortable if a boy is too hesitant, cautious, or vulnerable—let alone sheds a tear. I see this even with my own twenty-first-century feminist husband, who regularly roughhouses with my son to "toughen him up" and tells me to let him cry it out when he's screaming at night. I once asked him if he would do the same if Shaan were a girl and he immediately responded, "Of course not."

Of course, these beliefs don't vanish just because we grow up. If anything, the pressure on women to be perfect ramps up as life gets more complex. We go from trying to be perfect students and daughters to perfect professionals, perfect girlfriends, perfect wives, and perfect mommies, hitting the marks we're supposed to and wondering why we're overwhelmed, frustrated, and unhappy. Something is just *missing*. We did everything right, so what went wrong?

When you're writing a book about women and perfectionism,

you start to see it everywhere. In airports, at coffee shops, at conferences, at the nail salon . . . pretty much anywhere I went, I'd strike up a conversation on the topic and women would invariably sigh or roll their eyes knowingly, nod or laugh in recognition, or get sad as they shared a personal story. They'd tell me how their daily lives are ruled by a relentless inner drive to do everything flawlessly, from curating their Instagram feed to pleasing their partner (or struggling to find the "perfect" partner) to raising all-star kids who are also well adjusted (and who go straight from a year of breastfeeding to eating homemade, organic meals); from staying in shape and looking "good for their age" to striving ceaselessly to be the best in the office, in their congregation or volunteer group or community, in Soul-Cycle and CrossFit classes, and everywhere else.

So many women of all ages opened up to me about unfulfilled life dreams or ambitions they harbor because they're too afraid to act on them. Regardless of ethnicity, profession, economic circumstances, or what town they call home, I was struck by how many of their experiences were the same. You'll hear from many of them throughout this book.

But first, I want to show you all the ways the drive to be perfect got ingrained in us. What follows in this chapter is a glimpse into how our perfectionism took root as girls, how it shaped us as women, and how it colored every choice we've made along the way. We need to understand how we got here so we can thoughtfully navigate our way out. This is the beginning of the road map that leads us off a path of regret and onto one where we fully express who and what we most want to be.

The Origins of Perfectionism

Where along the way did we trade in our confidence and courage for approval and acceptance? And why?

The categorization of girls as pleasant and agreeable starts almost as soon as they're born. Instinctually, whether we realize it or not, we ascribe certain expectations to infants we see in pink or blue; babies in pink are all sugar and spice, babies in blue are tough little men. But it turns out that we even make assumptions when there are no other telltale signs of gender. One study showed that when infants are dressed in a neutral color, adults tend to identify the ones who appear upset or angry as boys, and those they described as nice and happy as girls. The training begins before we're even out of onesies.

In girls, the drive to be perfect shows up and bravery shuts down somewhere around age eight—right around the time when our inner critic shows up. You know the one I'm talking about: it's that nitpicking voice in your head that tells you every which way you aren't as good as others . . . that you blew it . . . that you should feel guilty or ashamed . . . that you *fucking suck* (I don't know about yours, but my inner critic can be a bit harsh).

Catherine Steiner-Adair is a renowned clinical psychologist, school consultant, and research associate at Harvard Medical School. She works with hundreds of girls and young women across the country and has seen firsthand how devastating perfectionism can be.

At around the age of eight, she says, kids start to see that ability and agility matter. "That's the age when girls start to develop different interests, and they want to bond with others who do what they like to do. Along with that awareness of differences comes an inner sense of who and what is better."

This is also the age in which kids begin to be graded, ranked, and told their scores—whether it's in soccer, math, or music, Steiner-Adair explains. "If you're told you're not as good, it requires a great deal of courage and self-esteem to try something. This sets the stage for getting a C means you're bad at it, and you don't like it. That feeds the lack of courage."

As girls get older, their radars sharpen. Around this age, they start to tune in when their moms compare themselves to others ("I wish I looked like that in jeans") or talk about other girls or women critically ("She should *not* be wearing that"). Suddenly they're caught up in this dynamic of comparison, and naturally redirect their radar inward to determine where they fall on the spectrum of pretty or not, bright or average, unpopular or adored.

These impulses are so deeply ingrained in us as adults and parents that we don't realize how much we inadvertently model them for our girls. Catherine shared a story from her own life that brought the point home. When her daughter was in third grade, she and some classmates overheard one mom say to another girl, "You have such pretty hair." Some of the girls stopped dead in their tracks and furrowed their brows as if to wonder, *So is my hair pretty or ugly?* And so it begins.

The Overpowering Need to Please

Like most women, I was taught from an early age to be helpful, obedient, and care for other people's needs, even to put them above my own. When my parents told me not to date until I was sixteen, I didn't. When they said no makeup, or showing cleavage, or staying out past 10 p.m., I obeyed. I complied at all times with the behavior my family expected of me. In our Indian household, one greeted elders by touching their feet as a sign of respect; if I came home from school with a friend and found an older auntie there having tea, I would never dream of disrespecting my parents by not doing it, although I was mortified in front of my friend. At family dinners, my sister and I set and cleared the table, never questioning why our male cousins didn't have to take a turn. Even though I would have much rather been outside playing with my friends, I always agreed to babysit my neighbor's (bratty) kids. That's just what helpful girls my age did.

Thus began my lifelong mission to be the perfect daughter, the perfect girlfriend, the perfect employee, the perfect mom. In this I know I'm not alone. We go from yes-girls to yes-women, caught in a never-ending cycle of constantly having to prove our worth to others—and to ourselves—by being selfless, accommodating, and agreeable.

A great example of how powerful the people-pleasing impulse can be comes from an experiment about lemonade. Yes, lemonade. ABC News, with the help of psychologist Campbell Leaper from the University of California, gave groups of boys and girls a glass of lemonade that was objectively awful (they added salt instead of sugar) and asked how they liked it. The boys immediately said, "Eeech . . . this tastes disgusting!" All the girls, however, politely drank it, even choked it down. Only when the researchers pushed and asked the girls why they hadn't told them the lemonade was terrible did the girls admit that they hadn't wanted to make the researchers feel bad.

The need to please people often shows up in the way girls scramble to give the "right" answer. Ask a girl her opinion on a topic and she'll do a quick calculation. Should she say what the teacher/parent/friend/boy is looking for her to say, or should she reveal what she genuinely thinks and believes? It usually comes down to whichever she thinks will be more likely to secure approval or affection.

Girls are also far more likely than boys to say yes to requests even when they really want (and even need) to say no. Remember, being accommodating has been baked into their emotional DNA. When I ask girls what they do if a friend asks them to do her a favor they really don't want or have time to do, nearly all say they would do it anyway. Why? Hallie, a freckle-faced fourteen-year-old, neatly summed it up with a "duh, that's so obvious" shrug: "No one wants their friends to think she's a bitch. I mean, *no one.*"

The internal pressure to say yes only gets stronger as we grow up. Like Dina, who works long hours as an attorney but somehow felt guilted into agreeing to be her son's class parent. So many of us give our time, attention, maybe even money, to people or causes that are not a priority to us because we don't want to hurt anyone's feelings (mostly, though, because we don't want them to think badly of us).

Boys, and the men they become, rarely feel this way. Janet, a forty-four-year-old manager at a clothing store, cringes anytime she reads an email that her husband, a general contractor, sends for work because she thinks his directness sounds harsh. He bluntly asks for what he needs or states his opinion, never softens critical feedback, and signs his emails without any salutations. No "best wishes" or even "thanks." When she once suggested he soften the tone of an email to a vendor he worked with so as to not piss him off, he told her, "It's not my job to be liked. It's my job to get my point across."

She, on the other hand, peppers her emails to her boss and coworkers with friendly lead-ins, praise, and, occasionally, a smiley face emoji. She reads over every email at least three times, editing and reediting it before she hits send. "My husband thinks I'm being neurotic when I do that," Janet told me. "I think I'm being thorough. But if I'm being really honest, I'd say I'm being cautious so I don't annoy or offend anyone."

I work with an executive coach who tells me all the time that being liked is overrated. She does not say this to the über-successful male CEOs she coaches; she doesn't have to. After all, their role models are men like Steve Jobs and Jeff Bezos who are notorious for not being people pleasers, so they don't give a damn whether they're liked or not.

Despite my coach's urgings, I *do* worry about being liked. Running for office, especially in New York City, I built a pretty tough skin when it comes to public criticism. But on a day-to-day level, I care whether my team likes me. I care a lot. I want them to think I'm the most amazing boss they've ever had—which makes giving them critical feedback really hard. I do it, because I know I have to be the CEO, but *ugh*. In my personal life, I get completely twisted up inside if I have a disagreement with a friend or if I sense my parents or husband are upset with me. I've definitely spent nights worrying about how a colleague, an acquaintance—even a complete stranger!—may have interpreted something I've said, and I've soft-pedaled way too many times when I really should have ripped someone a new one.

Just yesterday a guy cut in front of me in line while I was buying a sandwich and even though I was pissed, I didn't say a word because I didn't want to be rude—and this was someone I didn't even know and would likely never see again. And I too have been guilty of saying nice things even when I secretly think the exact opposite, so as to not offend (hello, salty lemonade). Haven't we all?

The result of all this toxic people pleasing is that your whole life can quickly become about what others think, and very little about what *you* genuinely want, need, and believe—let alone what you deserve. We've become conditioned to compromise and shrink ourselves in order to be liked. The problem is, when you work so hard to get everyone to like you, you very often end up not liking yourself so much. But once you learn to be brave enough to stop worrying about pleasing everyone else and put yourself first (which you will!), that's when you become the empowered author of your own life.

The "Softer" Sex

One sunny Saturday morning in late May, I sat on a bench in a playground in downtown Manhattan watching my husband, Nihal, and our then sixteen-month-old son, Shaan, play. Or, rather, I was watching my son bop from the monkey bars to the jungle gym and back again while Nihal stood a decent distance away and watched. Shaan's shirt was smeared with strawberry ice cream and his nose was filled with boogers, but he didn't care—and neither did I. Still new to the whole vertical coordination thing, Shaan toppled over a couple of times as he waddled from one end of the playground to another; each time, rather than run to his rescue, Nihal calmly waited for him to get up and keep going. At one point, I looked over and saw him coaxing Shaan, who was a little scared, down the big slide. "You can do this . . . you're a big boy . . . you're not afraid!"

Nearby, a few older boys were play-fighting using sticks as swords and chasing one another. Lots of happy hollering and a sea of dirty, scabby knees and elbows: a classic case of grade-school boys at play.

Meanwhile, over at the sandbox, five girls who looked to be around three years old were playing quietly. No ice-cream-smeared shirts or booger-encrusted noses there. Wearing cute coordinated outfits, they took turns scooping piles of sand to make a pretend cake, while their moms watched intently from a few feet away. In a ten-minute span, three of the five moms jumped up from their perches and climbed into the sandbox—one to straighten her daughter's headband and another to reprimand her daughter for being "rude" by taking the shovel from another girl. The third mom rushed to her daughter's aid after her sand "cake" fell over and hurriedly helped her daughter rebuild it while making soothing noises and wiping the tears from the girl's face. When the cake was fixed, the little girl smiled and her mom beamed with pride, "There's my happy girl!"

You can't make this stuff up.

Nearly everything I'd read, researched, witnessed, and interviewed experts about over the past year was playing out right in front of me. Go figure: a classic illustration of how boys are socialized to be brave and girls to be perfect, right here on a little asphalt playground less than ten minutes from my apartment.

At the same time we're applauding our girls for being nice, polite, and perfect, we are also telling them in not-so-subtle ways that bravery is the domain of boys. What I saw that day on the playground reminded me of another scene I'd witnessed just a few months earlier in Shaan's swim class. Parents were encouraging their timid sons to "be tough," and shouting with glee when their boys jumped into the deep end. If one of the little girls in the class was afraid to jump in, however, her fears were met with soft, reassuring coos: "It's okay, honey . . . just take my hand . . . you don't have to get your face wet." This one really made no sense to me; I mean, how do you go swimming without getting wet?

This isn't just casual observation on my part. Studies

show that parents provide much more hands-on assistance and words of caution to their daughters, while their sons are given encouragement and directives from afar and then left to tackle physical challenges on their own. We start with protecting girls physically, and the coddling continues on from there.

So many of these patterns are perpetuated because as parents, we're punished socially for violating them. A woman named Kelly told me a story about a group excursion she took to Oregon with her son and daughter, along with several other families. After taking a mountain bike ride, they hiked up a cliff where the rocks create a natural slide into the water. Their guide, Billy, helped all the kids out onto the rocks and offered them a push down the slide. The boys all went right away, but Kelly's usually courageous daughter was nervous. Instead of encouraging her the way he had done with the boys—that is, by just giving them a little shove—Billy helped her off the cliff and gently assured her that she didn't have to go if she didn't want.

Meanwhile, Kelly, knowing that her daughter is usually fearless, was hollering from the bottom, "Go, Ellie!" When it became clear that Billy wasn't going to give her a nudge as he did for the boys, she screamed up the cliff, "JUST PUSH HER!" Everyone around was *horrified*. "Every adult on the tour gave me the side-eye," she remembers. "They didn't even try to hide their judgment about how I was encouraging someone to push my daughter to be brave. We're not supposed to do that to our daughters."

The belief that boys are tough and resilient while girls are vulnerable and need to be protected is both deeply and widely held. In 2017, the World Health Organization released a groundbreaking study done in partnership with Johns Hop-

kins Bloomberg School of Public Health. Across fifteen countries, from the United States to China to Nigeria, these very
gender stereotypes proved to be universal and enduring; and
the study found that children buy into this myth at a very
early age.

This "girls are softer" mentality extends beyond the playground, often straight into the classroom. One problem is
what girls focus on when they're given difficult feedback.
When girls are told they got a wrong answer or made a mistake, all they hear is condemnation, which sears like a flaming
arrow straight through the heart. They go straight from "I did
this wrong" to "I suck" to "I give up," rarely stopping at "Oh,
I see how I could do this better next time."

The bigger problem, however, is how adults respond.
To spare the girls' fragile feelings, we naturally temper anything that sounds too critical. More protection, more soft-
pedaling, more steering girls to what's "safe," more feeding
the self-fulfilling prophecy of girls as vulnerable. But if they
are constantly shielded from any sharp edges, how can they
be expected to build any resilience to avoid falling apart later
in life if (more like when) they run up against real criticism
or setbacks?

Boys, on the other hand, have repeatedly been shown to
bounce right back from criticism or negative feedback, so we
don't hold back. Brad Brockmueller, one of our Girls Who
Code instructors who teaches at the Career and Technical
Academy in Sioux Falls, readily admits that teachers feel they
need to tailor their feedback differently for boys and girls. "If
boys try something and get it wrong, they'll just keep trying and coming back," he said. "With girls, I have to focus
on what they got right first before telling them what doesn't
work, then encourage them." He recalls the time he had the

class making network cables and one of the girls got frustrated because she couldn't get it right. "She wanted to give up, but to keep her going, I had to reinforce how much of it she'd gotten right and how close she was to nailing it. Some of the boys came up to me with a cable that wasn't well done and I literally took a scissors and chopped off the end and said, 'Nope, not right; try again.' And they did."

Brad also currently coaches the girls' basketball team, which he's found to be much different from his experience coaching the boys. "With girls you have to stay constantly positive," he says. "If you go negative or critical, they just shut down and there's nothing you can do to pull them out of that funk. If boys lose, it's just a game . . . they figure they'll play hundreds of games in their high school career, they'll get over one loss. For girls, a loss is personally defeating. They think, 'Why am I even playing basketball at all?' "

Debbie Hanney is the principal of Lincoln Middle School, an all-girls school in Rhode Island. She sees many parents caught between wanting to teach their daughters resilience and wanting to shield them from the sting of failure. She describes how, when a girl gets a 64 on a test, parents immediately swoop in and focus on how their daughter can get that grade up or take the test over. "We try to explain it as one thing on the continuum, but parents are understandably nervous in this day and age. It's hard trying to encourage them to let their daughters fail," she says.

It's deep stuff, this urge to protect and shield girls from disappointment and pain. Even more profound are the long-term effects, which many of us feel today as grown women. If we think about how horrified we are by the idea of failing, whether it's a serious rejection or a little mistake that we ruminate over for days, we can see how avoiding disappointment in our early life sliced into our resilience. We just didn't get the practice we needed to give us the bounceback that life demands. The good news here is that it's never too late. We can build resilience through bravery, and in later chapters, I'll show you how.

Perfection or Bust

When girls first walk into our Girls Who Code program, we immediately see their fear of not getting it right on full display. Every teacher in our program tells the same story.

At some point during the early lessons, a girl will call her over and say she is stuck. The teacher will look at her screen and the girl's text editor will be blank. If the teacher didn't know any better, she'd think her student had spent the past twenty minutes just staring at the screen.

But if she presses "undo" a few times, she'll see that her student wrote code and deleted it. The student tried. She came close. But she didn't get it exactly right. Instead of showing the progress she made, she'd rather show nothing at all.

Perfection or bust.

Dr. Meredith Grossman is a psychologist on the Upper East Side of Manhattan. With its concentration of highly competitive private schools, it is arguably the high-pressure-school capital of the world. She works with many girls to help them manage anxiety, and I asked her to tell me a little about what she sees on a daily basis.

"What's fascinating is the extreme amount of work they put into everything, and how much they underestimate their performance," she said. "I work with a lot of highly intelligent girls, and the quality of their writing is superior to what most adults can produce. But I constantly hear, 'I couldn't possibly turn that in.' They write and rewrite five times. They'd rather ask for an extension than turn something in they think isn't perfect."

As soon as one paragraph or paper is polished to perfection, it's on to the next. There's no break in the cycle because it's rare that their extreme efforts don't pay off. "Perfection begets more perfection," Meredith explained. "Every time a student overstudies or rewrites something five times and gets a good grade, it gets reinforced that she needs to do that again to succeed."

For every girl who writes and rewrites her papers until she's bleary-eyed, there's a woman who reads (and rereads, and rereads . . .) an email, report, or even a simple birthday card before sending it to make sure it hits precisely the right note, or spends weeks planning the ideal dinner party or a family trip to make everyone happy, or changes her outfit six times before leaving the house. We revise, rework, and refine to get things just right, often to a point of obsession or frustration that takes us out of the game.

Whether I'm speaking at a private school in New York City or at a community center in Scranton, Pennsylvania, I ask the girls in the audience the same question: "How many of you strive to be perfect?" Almost without exception, 99 percent of the hands in the room shoot up. Not with embarrassment—with smiles. They *know* they're trying to be perfect and are proud of it! They're rewarded for that behavior so they see it as a virtue. We heap praise on our girls for getting good grades, being well behaved and well liked, and for being good listeners, polite, cooperative, and all the other qualities that earn them gold stars on their report cards. We tell them that they're smart and talented, pretty and popular. They respond to these messages positively and wear them like a badge of honor. Is it any wonder that they see perfection as the only acceptable option?

In perfect-girl world, being judged harshly by their peers is the ultimate mortification; many girls and young women told me they won't post pictures on social media that are anything short of perfectly posed and meticulously edited. They'll take and retake a picture dozens of times to make sure it's flattering. One seventeen-year-old who suffers from a mild case of scleroderma, an autoimmune disease that caused a small patch of hardened skin on her forehead, admitted that she will anxiously spend up to an hour trying to take the perfectly arranged selfie in which her "patch" is 100 percent concealed by her long bangs. To make matters even more agonizing, the new thing is to go in the complete opposite direction and post "no filter" photos, which becomes a whole other level of pressure to capture that selfie that's "perfectly imperfect" *without* filters.

Girls will freely admit that they're afraid to blemish their records, so they don't take classes they aren't certain they can get a high grade in—no matter how interested they are in the subject. This continues through college, as they automatically close doors to career paths they could potentially love. It's not a coincidence that male economics majors outnumber women three to one; research done by Harvard economics professor Claudia Goldin revealed that women who earn B's in introductory economics are far more likely to switch majors than those who earn A's (while their male counterparts stick with it, B's be damned).

Appearing stupid is a huge concern. In perfect-girl world, being judged harshly by one's peers is the ultimate mortification; and it's been shown to be one of the main barriers girls face when they think about doing anything brave. For Destiny, math had always been a challenge. But the boys in her middle school made her feel far worse about it. "I'd be up at the board for a long time trying to work out a problem, and they'd say something like, 'You're so dumb,' or they'd laugh, and I'd get all flustered. It made me not even want to try to do math anymore. Why put all this effort in, just to get it wrong, and get yelled at by the boys?"

I know how she feels. When I was in law school at Yale, I remember sitting in my constitutional law class wanting desperately to contribute but feeling too intimidated. I mean, I was a girl from Schaumburg, Illinois, who was one of the first in my community to go on to an Ivy League grad school. All my classmates seemed so smart and impeccably articulate, and I didn't want to seem stupid in comparison. So I'd write out in my notebook exactly what I wanted to say, then I'd rewrite it three, four, a dozen times. By the time I worked up the courage to raise my hand, class was usually over.

Of course, the fears of not measuring up extend beyond the classroom. Amanda wanted to try lacrosse in high school but didn't because she's "not athletic." She summed up in two sentences a familiar sentiment I heard expressed in so many different varieties: "I just felt like if I couldn't do it well, I didn't want to do it at all."

It's important to understand that for girls, failure is defined as anything that is less than the proverbial A+. It's black and white: you either totally rock or totally suck. To them, failure isn't just painful—it's colossal, devastating, and to be avoided at all costs. So if they can't rock it, they skip it.

The Fixed Mindset

When Amanda declared that she didn't dare try lacrosse, she fell victim to a type of thinking that Stanford psychologist

Carol Dweck famously outlined in her brilliant book *Mindset*. In a nutshell, Dweck identified two different belief systems about ability and intelligence.

The first is a *fixed mindset*. A person with a fixed mindset believes that their abilities are innate and unchangeable. You're either smart or you aren't, talented or untalented, athletic or not at all, and there's not much you can do about it. The other is a *growth mindset*, which is based on the belief that abilities can be developed and cultivated through effort. Regardless of whatever natural level of ability or talent you are born with, you can learn skills and improve.

These are the hallmarks of a fixed mindset:

- An urgency to prove oneself again and again.
- Deep concern about making mistakes and failing.
- A reluctance to expose deficiencies.
- Seeing imperfections as shameful.
- The expectation that one will do well on something right away and if one doesn't, the loss of interest or self-admonishment for having put in the effort.
- The tendency to see failures as a measure of one's worth and allowing those failures to define the person.
- Being solely focused on the outcomes. It doesn't matter what one achieved or learned along the way. Not hitting the final mark means failure. And failure means that one isn't smart, talented, or good enough.

Sound familiar?

When you tell someone with a fixed mindset that they are smart or talented, they etch these messages into the "this is how I am" truth in their minds. That sounds like good, positive self-esteem building, but the problem is that after being showered with such praise of their perceived innate abilities, they fall to pieces when they encounter setbacks. Why? Because they take any failure, however insignificant, as a sign that maybe they aren't as innately smart or talented as they thought.

A fixed mindset also holds us back from trying anything outside our comfort zone. How many times have you begged off doing something spontaneous and potentially fun with, "I'm just not adventurous," or turned down an invitation or opportunity because "that's just not who I am"? That's the fixed mindset at work.

Not surprisingly, girls are more prone to a fixed mindset than boys. This is partially because, as Dr. Dweck's research showed, parents and teachers tend to give boys more "process praise," meaning they reward them for putting in effort, trying different strategies, sticking with it, and improving, rather than for the outcome. In the absence of this kind of process praise, girls come to believe that if they can't get something right away, they're dumb. You can see how this impacts us later in life, as we take even the smallest daily mistakes as indicators of fundamental limitations. We forget to pick up the school supplies our kid asked for = we're bad moms. We get a ticket for a broken taillight that we'd been meaning to take care of = we're idiots. We see a failure as a definitive condemnation of our worth, rather than seeing ourselves and our abilities as works in progress.

The single best example I can point to of girls being trapped in a fixed mindset is in relation to STEM subjects (science, technology, engineering, math). As you might imagine, being the founder of an organization that teaches coding to girls, I hear the refrain "I'm just not good at math" a lot. Like Destiny, who cringed when the boys made fun of her for taking so long up at the board to solve a math problem, or like the girls who delete their work in coding classes, it isn't a lack of interest or capacity in these subjects that scares them off, but a perception that they're fundamentally bad at it. After being told outright—or subtly, through the micromessages we'll talk about in the next chapter—that boys are naturally better at math and computing (they aren't) and that girls are innately more suited for humanities (again, not true), they believe to their core that their abilities in these subjects—or lack thereof—are carved in stone.

Of course, they aren't. Carol Dweck points out that no one is born with a fixed mindset; in fact, we all come prewired with a desire to learn and grow. It's only once children begin to evaluate themselves (I'm smart/not smart) that they become afraid of challenges. Thankfully, as adults, we *can* undo that long-ago wiring by taking on the practice of bravery in the here and now.

Silenced Voices

On a gray afternoon in late January, I sat around a conference table talking with a group of high school girls from Harlem. Kim, the most opinionated of the group, sat up straight with unusual presence for a girl her age. All outward signs pointed to a confident, secure young woman so I was surprised when she shared her inner reality with us.

"I feel like whenever girls speak up for themselves, we get slapped down for it because it seems like we're being bossy," she said. "Especially if I stand up for myself as a black woman specifically, boys really don't get it. If a boy does it, it's like he's a boss man . . . but if it's me, I'm just an angry black woman. Boys will say dumb stuff like they only like light-skinned

girls . . . if I speak up to them, they tell me I just like to com-
plain and dismiss me."

"But you're pretty outspoken," I said. "Does their reaction
have an effect on you?"

"Please . . . you think I want to be smacked down for what
I think all the time?" Kim put on a good show of sound-
ing tough as she spoke, but I could hear a tiny tremor in her
voice. Her bravado didn't quite match the vulnerability peek-
ing through. After a beat and a few hard blinks of her eyes,
she explained that she just found it easier to stay quiet than
deal with the boys trying to put her down. "Everyone thinks
I don't care but I do," she continued. "I feel like anything I say
will just turn into a whole big thing, and then everyone will
get into it and turn on me, too, so I don't bother."

The other seven girls around the table all nodded knowingly. Don't be too much, don't say too much, and definitely
don't say anything that makes you sound angry or bossy. Got it.

From the time girls are young, they're trained to keep a lid
on anger in the face of an affront, unlike boys who are trained
to stand up for themselves, or retaliate. This explains why
girls (and women) will do almost anything to avoid rocking
the boat, and why they choose to downsize their personal
power and swallow negative feelings, rather than be seen as
boastful or face the horror of confrontation. Praised on the
one hand by parents and teachers for being polite, agreeable,
and "well behaved" and, on the other, punished by their peers
for speaking out, the docility girls are rewarded for as children
translates directly into a lifelong habit of suppressing their instinct to speak up and take a risky stand. Mansplaining and
dominance plays aside, it's not surprising that findings show
women speak less than 75 percent of the time than men do in
conference meetings.

Modesty—another prized virtue for girls—also plays a hand in keeping us quiet and meek. I recently heard a story about a sixth-grade graduation ceremony in suburban Ohio, where a handful of kids were presented with awards for academics or leadership. A mom of one of those students described the scene for me: When a boy won an award, he would saunter up to the stage with a swagger. More than one "dabbed"–a hip-hop dance move that lots of pro athletes use in moments of triumph. When a girl won, she would throw her hands up to her face feigning a look of shocked surprise as if to say, *Who, me? You want to give an award to me?*

So why don't girls dab, too? Because if being a confrontational bitch is the first cardinal sin for girls, being seen as conceited runs a close second. So they downplay, demur, and hold back. Add ten, twenty, thirty years to this story and we see that modesty devolved into an uncomfortable meekness. It makes us squeamish to self-promote our professional accomplishments (possibly because we know other women will judge us for it, just like we'd judge them), yet our male colleagues proudly trumpet theirs. We underestimate our abilities and hold off going for a job unless we are *absolutely* sure we're 100 percent qualified, while men charge ahead if they come in around 60 percent qualified. We undervalue our contribution to a collaborative project and give more credit to our male teammates, as a fascinating study from Michelle Haynes of the University of Massachusetts and Madeline Heilman of New York University revealed.

At age thirty-eight, Vanessa is a successful dermatologist. She's one of those people who radiates competence, so you wouldn't think that she'd fall prey to the same trepidation about touting her accomplishments. Yet on a routine visit to get her teeth cleaned, her (older, male) dentist, upon hearing what she does for a living, immediately launched into a story about his son who was a resident in medical school. "I just sat there as he went on and on about how I should call his son because he could probably give me some good advice about the business," she said. "I was thinking, *huh?* Never mind that I own my own practice with three associates, or that I've been listed as a top doctor in national magazines. I still sat there not feeling brave enough to tell him it was probably his son who should be calling *me* for advice."

Caught in the "double bind" that says we need to be assertive and confident if we want to get ahead, but knowing we'll get heaped with disapproval if we do, we tread lightly. When someone compliments us, we humbly deflect. This is one I definitely struggle with. Every time someone introduces me before a speech, they inevitably read off the awards I've won. Then I'll get up there and make a joke about how my dad probably put them up to it. I'm pretty sure no guy would ever do that.

Quiet. Contained. Modest. Diligent. Likable. Easy to get along with. You can see how all these accolades might have earned us high praise in girlhood but aren't necessarily doing us any favors as grown women.

Now, if you're a parent reading this and thinking, *I've totally screwed up my daughter*—or are getting ready to blame your own parents for doing a number on you—let me stop you right there. The pressures on girls to be perfect does NOT all come down on the parents. It's important that we understand how ingrained these cultural norms are, and how hard it is for them *not* to become internalized. As you'll read about in the next chapter, more and more it's about the messages girls are getting from the culture we live in, and their parents are caught with them in the same tangled net. But don't despair—all hope is not lost, for you or for your daughter! As psychologist Dr. Meredith Grossman says, "It's not about parents screwing up. It's about becoming aware of these internalized beliefs and making different choices."

We *can* reverse and relearn these habits—and help our daughters do the same—with just a little awareness and practice. And in Part Three I'll share my best tips, ideas, and strategies for doing exactly that.

2

The Cult of Perfection

We are living in the era of girl power. From fiery Beyoncé anthems to powerhouse athletes like Serena Williams to badass literary and on-screen heroines like Katniss Everdeen and Wonder Woman, our culture is on a crusade to rally girls and tell them they can be and do it all. Of course we want our girls to know they can accomplish anything and everything they set their minds to! Right?

All this "positive" messaging, however, turns out to have a dark side. We hold up these larger-than-life women as role models with the goal of empowerment, but for many girls it lands as crushing pressure to excel in everything. We may be saying, "You can do and be anything," but they hear, "You *have to* do and be everything" What we might see as inspiration, they take as expectation.

My friend Rachel Simmons, one of the country's leading experts on girls and the bestselling author of *The Curse of the Good Girl*, points to this mentality as a factor contributing to the significant mental health crisis we see in today's young women. Rates of depression and anxiety are skyrocketing, and she says part of the problem is the role conflict girls today live with on a daily basis. "We've only added on to what it means to be a successful girl," she explains. "We didn't update it. If you're expected to be in the library for six hours studying, how are you also expected to have a really great body and great weekend plans?" Now they need to be nice, but also fierce; polite but also bold; cooperative but trailblazing; strong but also pretty. All this plus, in a culture that lauds effortless perfection, making it look like they're not trying—not even a bit.

Sophie is a perfect example. At fifteen, she is tall and lanky, with unblemished skin and a gorgeous smile that reveals two perfect rows of straight, white teeth. She's a star soccer player, she's been on the varsity team since she was in seventh grade, played Belle in her eighth-grade production of *Beauty and the Beast*, and got elected to the student council in ninth grade—a highly competitive and coveted post in her school. No surprise, she also gets straight A's. If you met her, you'd immediately be struck by how poised and articulate she is. Sophie's mom, Dina, is proud—but also very worried. She talked about how, despite her parents' urgings to take it easy, Sophie pushes herself relentlessly, waking up at the crack of dawn every morning to work out at the gym before she goes to school and often staying up until well past midnight to get her homework done (while wearing teeth whitening strips and acne-fighting face masks). To everyone else, it seems she's got it together; it's only her family that sees her cry nearly every night in frustration or sheer exhaustion. There isn't a single minute of Sophie's week or energy that isn't consumed with practicing, studying, working on student council issues, and perfecting her appearance— all without ever showing anyone other than her parents what really goes into her all-star packaging.

Be bold and brave . . . but make sure not to step on any toes or offend anyone. Go for what you want . . . as long as it's what we expect of you. Speak your mind . . . but make sure to smile when you do. Don't settle for less than you're worth . . . but ask for it nicely. Work hard . . . but make it look easy. This chapter is a glimpse inside how popular culture shapes the Perfect Girl, and what happens when she comes up against the confusing messages lobbed her way in the era of girl power.

Pretty like Mommy

Remember, we can't exclusively blame parents for creating generations of girls who are afraid of failing, or speaking up, or stepping out of line. The socially accepted gender beliefs that we—and our parents, and their parents—grew up with are so deeply etched into our psyches that it would be shocking if they *didn't* show up in our parenting. No, we need to look deeper into the culture we live in to find where the gender expectations are still flourishing and reseeding themselves in the next generation.

The cultural indoctrination starts early, with toys. Kids learn gender roles as early as thirty months old, and the toys and other merchandise they are nudged toward play a big role in that education. Studies show that play choices for boys and girls can have lasting effects on how they view themselves and their abilities, including what they believe they will be good at professionally when they grow up. It's almost hard to believe that child play can have that powerful effect, but it does. This goes way beyond trucks versus dolls or pink versus blue. The skills these toys teach set the gender narrative for what kids are "supposed" to like and excel at. The majority of toys and games created for boys like LEGOs and *Minecraft* are geared toward developing large motor skills like running and kicking and spatial skills, which are the 3-D visualization skills that are said to predict a child's achievement in STEM subjects. Toys for girls, on the other hand, generally build fine motor skills such as writing and making crafts, language development, and social interaction. Just in case you're thinking we've evolved past this, research from scholar Elizabeth Sweet at UC Davis shows that the gender marketing of toys is even *more* pronounced today than it was fifty years ago, when gender discrimination and sexism were as baked into our culture as apple pie.

We can't talk about the influence of toys without mentioning princesses. The effect the princess movies and paraphernalia has on girls has been hotly debated in recent years. Of all the conversations and articles out there, it was a study done at Brigham Young University that resonated the most for me. Professor Sarah M. Coyne observed 198 preschoolers and found that a full 96 percent of the girls engaged with "princess culture" in one way or another. That's not a huge surprise, but more interesting is how, when she observed these same kids one year later, she found that the more these girls watched princess movies and played with princess toys, the more they exhibited stereotypical female behavior like playing nicely and quietly, avoiding getting dirty, or being submissive, passive, physically weak, and valuing qualities such as being nurturing, thin, pretty, and helpful. This sticks with us in profound ways, whether we know it or not. A related study showed that grown women who self-identify as "princesses" are less interested in working, give up more easily on challenges, and place higher value on superficial qualities like appearance.

Here's a particularly horrifying example of the messages girls receive from the world of toys. In 2014, Mattel released a Barbie book called *I Can Be a Computer Engineer*. Sounds empowering, right? But just wait. A few pages in, Barbie is having a conversation with her little sister, Skipper, about her robot puppy. Skipper says, "Your robot puppy is so sweet, can I play your game?" Barbie laughs and says, "I'm only creating the design ideas, I need Steven and Brian's help to turn it into a real game."

No, I'm not joking.

In a few words Barbie told girls: "You're not good enough or smart enough. Computers are a boy's thing so if you're going to build something technical, you're going to need their help." Leave it to Barbie to articulate some of the worst stereotypes that girls and women face when it comes to technology.

Eventually, playtime ends, but once we are done with toys, popular culture swooshes in to reinforce those gender constructs. For the majority of their waking hours, kids get bombarded with not-so-subtle images and messages about what's expected of them and how they are supposed to behave. These messages are everywhere they look, from fashion to movies to headline news. They see T-shirts in the window of Gymboree emblazoned either PRETTY LIKE MOMMY or SMART LIKE DADDY, and older teenage girls (whom they idolize) wearing the popular T-shirt from Forever 21 that says ALLERGIC TO ALGEBRA. They watch a viral video of a principal in South Carolina telling girls that unless they are a size 0 or 2, wearing leggings will make them look fat, and they hear about how presidential candidate Hillary Clinton was called a "nasty woman" for speaking boldly during a debate.

Needless to say, media and pop culture support a completely different reality for men. The images that boys see, from Marvel superhero movies to HBO's Silicon Valley, reinforce the same messages they get early in life: that they need to be daring and brave—physically, intellectually, and otherwise. That part isn't news, but this gets interesting when we see how we can trace a straight line from the messages men have absorbed about masculinity to their behavior. In one experiment, a researcher at University of California-Berkeley's Haas School of Business assessed his male subjects' risk tolerance with a gambling assignment, then had them read about "masculinity." Then he assessed them again. Just by *reading* about masculinity, the men, on average, become substantially more risk-tolerant than they had been before they read the material.

Comedian Amy Schumer highlighted the glaring differences in the messages boys and girls receive when she posted a photo on Instagram of a newsstand display showing *Girls' Life* and *Boys' Life* magazines right next to each other. The cover of *Boys' Life* said in bold letters "Explore Your Future" and was covered in photos of airplanes, firefighter helmets, microscopes, computers, and a human brain. The cover of *Girls' Life* featured a blond teenaged cutie surrounded by the taglines "Wake Up Pretty!," "Fall Fashion You'll Love: 100+ ways to slay on the first day," and "Best. Year. Ever. How to Have Fun, Make Friends and Get All A's." These might sound like quaint vintage headlines from the 1950s, but nope, they were proudly displayed without a hint of irony in 2017. Schumer's one-word comment neatly summed up the disgust I feel at this messaging: "No."

In my research for this book, I came across shortstoryguide .com, a website to help middle- and high school teachers and students find stories organized by theme. I typed in the word *bravery,* and of the seventeen stories listed, only four featured female protagonists. One was a princess who pretends to be ashamed for shooting a lion who lunged at her. Another, an aspiring astronomer, "has to help her family during the *charreada*, a Mexican-style rodeo. She is caught between her own desires and tradition." Meanwhile, the male protagonists in the remaining stories bravely confront violent gangs and a Nazi spy, go bear hunting and capture a Russian fort—free of shame, or family obligations.

A study done by the *Observer* in conjunction with Nielsen that assessed the one hundred most popular children's books of 2017 revealed a few casually sexist trends that stubbornly prevail in modern literature. Male characters are twice as likely to take leading roles while females play the sidekick; when the characters took the form of animals, the powerful, dangerous bears, dragons, and tigers were mostly male while the smaller and more vulnerable birds, cats, and insects were female. One-fifth of these books had no female characters at all.

Boys and girls will model themselves after what they see, and even what they don't see; as children's rights activist Marian Wright Edelman famously said, "You can't be what you can't see." There's a running theme in movies and on television about the nerdy guy who gets rejected and goes on to become Mark Zuckerberg, but there's no similar narrative for girls. We muse and debate why there aren't more girls interested in tech, but for one key factor, just look at the media's depiction of the "brogrammer"—the brilliant but socially awkward white guy in a hoodie who is obsessed with computers—that girls look at and say, "Um, no thanks. I don't want to be him."

Instead, they watch as women backstab and screech at each other while hurling over tables on *The Housewives of New Jersey* (and *New York* . . . and *Beverly Hills* . . . and *Atlanta* . .), and catfight their way to the final rose ceremony on *The Bachelor.*

Needless to say, these are not the best role models. Women who take power roles on-screen are usually depicted as cold, ruthless bitches, like Daenerys Targaryen on *Game of Thrones* and Cheryl Blossom on *Riverdale*, or as volatile crazies, like Frances McDormand as a grieving mother in *Three Billboards Outside Ebbing, Missouri* or Viola Davis as the formidable but unstable lawyer on *How to Get Away with Murder*.

When brave women are portrayed, they are often almost cartoonish in their depiction. Granted we had the amazing *Wonder Woman* movie, with a fierce and kind heroine who spoke twelve languages and literally did not know what the men were talking about when they told her she couldn't do something, but she was a superhero demigod who isn't exactly relatable on a human scale. Ditto for the lead character Bella in the *Twilight* series; she is a meek and needy mortal for the first three-quarters of the story, gaining supernatural strength and ferocity only after she morphs into a vampire. In the re-boot of the cult-classic movie *Tomb Raider*, Alicia Vikander's Lara Croft is a hard-bodied badass, but what real-life woman do you know who survives crash landings, parachutes off the top of a waterfall, and fights off machine gun attacks with a bow and arrow—all while managing to look camo-chic and sexy?

It's important to see people like you on-screen; the un-bridled, infectious joy we saw spread across the Internet after Jodie Whittaker was cast as the first female Dr. Who makes that clear. I decided I wanted to be a lawyer when I was thir-teen years old and saw actress Kelly McGillis kick serious ass in the movie *The Accused*. That was the first time I'd seen a female character in a movie go up against the big boys with-out pulling any punches. As my father and I left the movie theater, I turned to him and said, "Dad, I want to be her."

Think about all the young girls now who know who Katherine Johnson is because of *Hidden Figures*, and who now see being a NASA scientist as a possibility; these are the kinds of realistic role models we need for our girls.

#perfectgirl

Today, social media feeds the expectation of polished perfection, perhaps more than any other influence out there. Girls spend up to nine hours each day scrolling through endless feeds of their friends' flawless photos and posts—all doctored and edited to show the world how popular, carefree, smart, pretty, and cool they are.

Listening to some of the millennial women I met with, I couldn't help feeling terrified for them. It was astonishing to hear how relentless but utterly normalized the pressure is for them to project an image of perfection in their online life— way beyond what I even imagined. The "personal branding" phenomenon has become an obsession for them; taking and editing the perfect photo consumes their time and efforts like nothing else. I listened to a group of friends in their midtwenties debating who was most obsessed with getting the ideal shot; they were torn between Sasha, who practices her photo faces in front of the mirror every morning to see what works best with her "look" that day, and Layla, who routinely makes her boyfriend wake up with her at sunrise for an early morning photo shoot in order to capture herself in the flattering light of dawn. Other girls told me about how the "ugly" pictures that someone had posted of them haunt them, or about how they felt panicked that they need to positively document every little thing they do to stay relevant in the eyes of their peers.

Perhaps as a way to preserve a sense of their true self, they literally separate themselves into two identities: their polished, carefully cultivated online persona, and the real them. Many set up separate Instagram or Snapchat accounts, and it's only on their private accounts accessible to only their closest friends that they'll post pictures of themselves in sweatpants, share a goofy video of themselves learning to hoop dance (it's a thing), or post a message expressing grief when a relationship ends.

They know this identity splitting isn't healthy but feel powerless to do anything about it. Positive and pretty: that's what's expected of them, and if they don't comply, it's a one-way ticket to judgment city. Anna, a twenty-five-year-old grad student, used the phrase "negativity shaming" for the pushback they often get if they post anything too raw or real. Anna recounted a time when she was really down after a breakup with a boyfriend; she posted something about how down she was feeling, and instead of rallying around to support her, people commented that she was being "superintense." She removed the post within an hour.

It's safer and easier for girls to stick to the stuff that gets them the most likes, because that's their currency. The more you play by the rules, the more followers and likes you have, and in perfect-girl world, the more followers and likes you have, the more valuable you are. Curating is everything.

So is comparing. According to Catherine Steiner-Adair, psychologist and author of *The Big Disconnect: Parenting, Childhood, and Family Connection in the Digital Age*, it takes only nine minutes of scrolling through everyone else's profiles and pictures for girls' anxiety to spike. Their FOMO—fear of missing out—is very, very real. Every post of a fun gathering they weren't a part of makes them feel ostracized and unwanted, every perfectly polished photo causes paroxysms of inadequacy. They are constantly competing in the never-ending game of *who has more followers, whose photo got more likes,* and so on. Hey, I get it; I'm forty-two years old and I still find myself refreshing Instagram posts obsessively to see how many likes I have.

Catherine recalled one girl she interviewed who frequently goes on nice vacations with her family. After one such trip, she came back and told Catherine, "I had had this awesome vacation until I saw where this other girl went. I started thinking, Are we poor?" Catherine initially thought maybe she was kidding, but she wasn't. "First world problems, of course, but the idea that the comparison would dampen the meaning and enthusiasm of her great family vacation is terribly sad," Catherine commented.

Then there's the truly nasty side of all this, the fallout that can range from hurt and embarrassment to serious psychological damage. Unfortunately, the shaming and bullying are not new; even shaming and bullying on social media are not new. But what *is* new is how young it starts. These days, girls as young as seven years old are on Instagram, Facebook, and Snapchat, far too young to have developed strategies to cope with the judgment they find there. A mom of a ten-year-old told me a story about her daughter, whose first Instagram post two years ago was a photo of a bowl of chocolate ice cream. A girl from school commented, "Ewww . . . is that poop?" Shamed and embarrassed, her daughter hasn't posted a single thing since.

Another mom told me—her voice shaking through her tears—that her thirteen-year-old is struggling with an eating disorder, which began shortly after she posted a picture of herself in a bathing suit and towel; a group of boys screen-shot and circulated her picture with the tagline, "Pig in a blanket." I recently read about a horrifying Snapchat craze in which middle-school kids competed to see who could post the cruelest insult about another kid's personality or appearance.

As if girls didn't have enough to contend with, many can't resist logging on to sites like www.prettyscale.com to upload pictures of themselves and receive the answer promised by the site's provocative tagline, "Am I beautiful or ugly?" (the helpful small print below says, "Please do not start if you have low self-esteem or confidence issues," which would seem to rule out all preteen and teenage girls), or sites where you can post anonymously like ask.fm, Kik, and Voxer. Anonymous sites, not surprisingly, are fertile ground for the cruel cyberbullying that has been linked to tragic suicides, such as that of twelve-year-old Rebecca Ann Sedwick, who killed herself at the repeated urging of a group of middle-schooler bullies. It's heartbreaking. If ever there was a reason for us to learn to be brave, it is so we can teach the next generation how to make empowering choices in the face of messages and challenges like these.

Changing the Code

Looking at all this, we start to see how deeply we as adult women have been wired to play it safe and to color well inside the lines of perfection—and what it costs us. It's like a code that has been programmed into us, over many years of perfect-girl training. But take it from someone who actually now does know a thing or two about coding: all code can be revised and rewritten—including the one that dictates whether you choose the path of perfection, or bravery.

3

Perfection 3.0: When the Perfect Girl Grows Up

*I*f life were one long grade school, girls would rule the world."

This famous quote by Carol Dweck hits hard for all of us who were primed to be perfect girls. Of course, she's right: in school, the quest for perfection may have served us well, but in the real world, there are no straight A's. Inevitably, we grow up and discover very quickly that the rules have changed; suddenly, everything we've been taught backfires on us. The very same behaviors that used to pay off—like being nice, polite, and agreeable—suddenly end up costing us big-time, both literally and figuratively.

Playing nice doesn't get us the promotions or positions of power—and it certainly doesn't get us raises. Being overly accommodating lands us in situations and relationships we don't necessarily want to be in. Minding our manners and staying quiet leaves us feeling queasy knowing that we didn't tell our uncle Joe to shut it when he told one of his usual racist jokes, or call foul when a colleague took credit for an idea that was ours. Being sweet and ultrameticulous may earn us gold stars in the classroom, but by the time we hit the real world, those stars aren't exactly raining from the sky.

I once met a woman at a conference in California who

asked me, "How can I not strive to be perfect, when the world rewards perfection?" My answer to her was that maybe high school or college rewards perfection, but in the real world, it's different. The real world rewards bravery.

The pursuit of perfection may set us on a path that feels safe, but it's bravery that lets us veer off that "supposed to" path and onto the one we're authentically meant to follow. Perfection might win us points for popularity at the office, but it's bravery that lets us speak up and take a stand when we're hit with workplace sexism or harassment. Having a 4.0 GPA, an impeccable interview outfit, and a charming smile may get us in the door, but we need bravery to get our work recognized and advance beyond entry-level. Having perfect hair or the perfect body might land us a date, but it takes bravery to fall in love, and to do it all over again after our hearts have been broken. Trying to be the perfect mom might win us tacit approval on the playground, but it takes bravery to give our child the freedom to explore and make mistakes even though we desperately want to wrap them in bubble wrap to protect them forever. Perfection might feel good for a few fleeting moments, but bravery powers us through the difficult times and deep losses that can feel insurmountable. By being brave, not perfect, we get to create and live lives that don't just *look* good but are authentically, joyfully, messily, and completely ours.

How Did I Get Here?

"I didn't know until I was in my late twenties that I had choices in life," Ruth told me. She and I met while sitting side by side at a nail salon and struck up one of those unusually intimate conversations the way one sometimes randomly does with a complete stranger. Ruth got the message when she was young that an appropriate path for her was to become a teacher, get married, have kids, and then stay home to raise them. It didn't even dawn on her that she had other options—that is, until she was twenty-eight and a friend of hers joined the Peace Corps and moved to South America. "All of a sudden I thought, wait a minute . . . you mean I can do that?!" At age sixty-two, Ruth says she sometimes wonders what turns her life might have taken if she'd looked within and asked herself what she really wanted.

All the lessons we learn as little girls have real consequences on our life choices. So many of us have been trained to please others—first and foremost our parents—and so we follow the "expected" path without questioning if it's genuine for us. For some, like Ruth, it was getting married and having babies; for others, it's working tirelessly to get ahead. I see this a lot in young women raised by immigrant parents like Yara, whose dad grew up in a tiny city in Holland, with a bed that came down out of the wall. "When he moved their family here, there was no question—none—that I had to succeed at everything," she said. "It's what he came here for."

Julianne is first-generation Asian American. At the age of thirty-one, her family's disapproval of her life choices still stings. Her parents wanted her to become a doctor, but she got to a certain point in her training when she realized that wasn't how she wanted to spend her life, so she quit medicine and chose something that she really likes. In the back of her mind, she still wonders if she's a failure. "Anytime we have a family reunion," she told me, "there's a passive-aggressive undercurrent of 'Why did you choose that . . . could you not make the other path?'"

As a daughter of immigrant Indian parents, I totally relate. I thought if I did everything perfectly, got straight A's, was number one on my debate team, and valedictorian in college that all the sacrifices my parents made as refugees would be worth it. So, even though I secretly dreamed of being in public service, I went to work at a prestigious law firm, knowing it would earn my father's approval and praise. I hated my job, but I never let that show. I moved on and up to a high-paying job at a marquee-name financial firm, even though, for me, making money was only a means to an end (as in, to pay off my student loans and then go on to make a difference). Yet I made choice after choice like this, climbing up rung after rung on corporate ladders and making myself more miserable by the day. I spent all my free hours volunteering on political campaigns and giving back, but my day job in finance was completely disconnected from that. By the time I hit my early thirties, I was waking up most mornings curled in the fetal position, nursing the sick realization that my professional accomplishments were hollow. On paper you would have thought I had it made, but in reality I was way, way off my dream path.

That was a dark time in my life. My body and soul exhausted, I would often come home from work, change into comfy sweats, pour a glass of wine, turn on CNN, and just cry. I felt so stuck, not knowing what to do next and too scared to quit and free myself of the trap into which I'd fallen.

Until the day in 2008 when everything changed.

I remember so vividly it being one of those stifling hot August days in New York City, when the streets are gooey and standing on the subway platform makes you feel like you're being roasted. I was sitting in my hermetically sealed, frigidly air-conditioned office on the forty-eighth floor in the heart of

Midtown Manhattan in a fitted blue suit and four-inch heels that were killing me, trying to hold back the tears. Even my afternoon cappuccino tasted like fear and regret.

Less than two months earlier, I'd gone down to Washington, D.C., to offer support for my mentor Hillary Clinton as she gave her concession speech, ceding the 2008 Democratic nomination to then senator Barack Obama. I'd worked so hard volunteering on her campaign and, like so many others, felt disheartened and deflated. As I watched her speak, with tears streaming down my face, one message particularly stuck with me: that just because she failed doesn't mean that the rest of us should give up on our goals and dreams. I'd felt like she was speaking directly to me.

On that sweltering August day, I was replaying Hillary's speech in my head—as I had many times in the weeks since—when my phone pinged. It was Deepa, one of my best friends from law school. She knew me when I was still a bright-eyed graduate who believed I could do and be anything (she once walked in on me standing on her balcony practicing my presidential acceptance speech). I was never so happy to see a name light up on my phone! I quickly walked across the somber, hushed office into a windowless conference room in the back, closed the privacy blinds, kicked off those miserable heels, and picked up the call. The instant I heard Deepa's voice, the flood of tears came rushing out. I must have sounded a little nuts, sobbing and hiccupping as I told her I couldn't take this corporate job anymore . . . that I felt so empty . . . that my life had no purpose. She listened patiently until I was finished, paused, and then she said, simply and quietly, "Just quit." Maybe it was the inspiration from Hillary's strength and resilience, or hearing my best friend give me permission to do something I was terrified to do, but for the first time in as long as I could remember, I felt a glimmer of hope.

Shortly after that, I worked up the courage to tell my father that I wanted to quit my job and run for office. I was worried that he would say I shouldn't do it, which would have tapped right into my fear of his disapproval and made me give up on the idea entirely. When I dialed the phone to call him, I was so nervous that my hands were shaking; I *really* wanted this and didn't want anything to dim my excitement. You know what he said? "It's about time!" I never felt more proud to be my father's daughter than I did that day—and never wanted to kick myself harder for not going to him with my truth earlier. In the long run, I ended up making his American dream come true by going after my own.

I've met so many girls and women who made the same early mistakes I did. Like Melissa, an art history major who let her dream of being an artist waft away when she got married at twenty-two to her nice (but boring) Jewish boyfriend at the none-too-subtle urging of her religiously conservative parents. Almost on autopilot, she moved into a nice-size house and built a social life that was a mini-replica of theirs, including joining their synagogue. For a couple of years, she cheerfully played the part of gracious hostess and suburban wife, until the *Is this it?* feeling started to creep in. At twenty-five, she woke up one morning, looked around at her pristinely manufactured home and life, and thought, *Oh, hell no. This isn't where my story ends.* By her twenty-sixth birthday, Melissa was single, working for almost no money as a receptionist in an art gallery, and living in a tiny walk-up in Brooklyn. Was her life perfect? No. But she'd never been happier, because she'd let go of the expectation that it had to be.

The Myths of Perfection

Something interesting happened when I first started talking with women about perfection. I'd start off by asking them what I thought was a softball question to open the conversation: "Do you believe you need to be perfect?" I assumed the answer would obviously be yes, but nearly all of them said the exact opposite. I began to wonder if maybe I had it all wrong.

Then I realized they were answering the question from the very same style of thinking I was trying to unravel. They were giving me what they assumed was the *right* answer—the perfect answer—the answer that said *of course* they know that the pursuit of perfection is a demoralizing waste of time and energy. And yet all the stories I was hearing were telling a very different tale.

So from then on, when I spoke to groups of women, I changed the question. Instead of a binary yes or no question, I asked them instead to rate themselves on a scale of 1 to 10, 10 being that they were strongly driven to do everything in their lives to perfection. Just as I suspected, once I eliminated the suggestion of a "right" answer, a different picture began to emerge; the average answer was between 8 and 10. Once the floodgates began to open, I asked them if friends and family ever suggested that they were holding themselves to unreasonable standards; the answer was usually yes. I asked them if they believed that no matter what they did, they should've done better. That one scored an almost unanimous yes.

After talking to hundreds of women ranging from teenagers to senior citizens, from all backgrounds and walks of life, I've learned that perfectionism isn't simple or one-dimensional. It's a complex knot of lifelong beliefs, expectations, and fears. Our attitudes toward it are confusing and inconsistent; we nurture and feed it but wish like hell we could shake it. It can be an unforgiving taskmaster, naysayer, and critic all rolled into one. It greets us every morning as we stare in the mirror and keeps us awake, rehashing and ruminating over our mistakes, long into the night.

Sometimes perfectionism tells us that other people won't accept or value or love us unless we're perfect (what psychologists call "socially prescribed perfectionism"); other times it feels like we're the ones pushing ourselves to reach our own impossible standards ("self-oriented perfectionism"). Either way, it's a nagging presence that whispers in our ear, constantly reminding us of all the ways we failed others and ourselves.

Perfect-girl training aside, we're now smart, savvy women who intelligently know the pursuit of perfection is absurd. Yet it still rules our lives. Why? Because whether we're consciously aware of it or not, we still buy into some outdated myths about what being perfect will do for us. It's time to drag out these stubborn lies and kick them to the curb once and for all.

Myth #1: Polished Equals Perfect

From a very young age, we're taught that if we're polished on the outside, we'll get the perfect job, the perfect man, the perfect life. But polished doesn't equal perfect, and it definitely doesn't guarantee the happy ending. Believe me, I should know.

The delusion we harbor is that if we're perfect in how we look, sound, or behave, our secret—that we are actually *not* perfect—is safe. If we come off as flawless, we are beyond reproach: shielded from judgment or criticism. So we obsessively polish our veneer to keep any ugly insecurities, feelings, or flaws hidden from view.

Early on in my run for Congress, I was a wreck. A very worried wreck. I was nervous about whether I really had what it took to hold office. I felt like I needed to be an issues expert on everything from Iraq to potholes—what if someone asked me a question and I didn't have the answer? I already had my young age and lack of experience stacked against me; would I be seen as incompetent, not smart enough to do the job? I may have seemed tough and composed on the surface, but inside I was riddled with anxiety and self-doubt.

So I focused on the only thing I could control: my stump speech. Oh my god, I was so obsessed with that stump speech. I wrote and rewrote it dozens of times and memorized every word. I watched countless videos from great orators and rehearsed it over and over in my head while lying in bed, while brushing my teeth, while walking to the subway. I convinced myself that if I gave a flawless speech, I would appear flawless and spare myself the wrath of critics. I thought my flawless speech would be like a shield, that it would put me in control of how I was perceived. Needless to say, I was wrong. The haters still found plenty to hate on, from my words to my footwear. It wasn't until years later that I learned that the only thing that can truly protect me is my inner bravery.

For many of us, our appearance is our armor. If our outfit, hair, makeup, jewelry, shoes, and everything else are perfect, we feel in control. Yet this is an illusion that assumes we have power over how other people view and respond to us. One petite blond entrepreneur told me she gets her hair and makeup professionally done before she pitches to potential investors. "It's as if they can't fuck with me if I have a blowout," she said with a laugh. But the reality is that we're never really in control. Not of what people think of us in their private thoughts, and definitely not of what happens once we step away from the primping mirror or our carefully crafted notes. Of course anyone can fuck with you, with or without a blowout.

It wouldn't be possible to talk about women and perfectionism without mentioning the most obvious and insidious way we torture ourselves: our bodies. On average, a woman spends 127 hours per year fretting about her weight and how many calories she consumes. Over a lifetime, that adds up to *one full year* that we give to obsessing over the size and shape of our bodies. It's been estimated that between 80 and 89 percent of women are unhappy with their weight. Ten million women in this country have eating disorders. Even more disturbingly, the National Eating Disorders Association reports that 81 percent of *ten-year-old* girls are afraid of being overweight.

A few days following a packed focus group I did in New York City, I got an email from a participant named Marta who had sat quietly on the floor throughout the evening. But in her email she wrote candidly about how the whole experience had been very "meta" for her—here she was at an intimate gathering to talk about how perfectionism and fear hold us back, and she was too intimidated by the accomplished women sitting on the sofa across from her (she called them "the couch women") to speak up. I told Marta I was grateful to her for reaching out to me, as the story she then shared is one I think many of us can relate to in one way or another.

At a young age, she'd internalized the pressure to maintain a perfectly polished exterior from her mother, who had never, in the thirty-two years Marta had been on this earth, been outside of their house without a full face of makeup on. She was thin and very pretty and had always been in good shape, and Marta described to me how, in high school, boys would tell her that her mom was "hot," which made her feel nauseated and like she'd never measure up. "I was too big, my hair was too curly, my nose was too broken," she wrote.

These deep insecurities drove her to fix her nose when she was sixteen, which was also around when she stopped playing basketball, a game she had loved since childhood. "At seventeen, I tried straightening my hair (once) and literally cried about it," Marta recalled. "At eighteen, I left for college and immediately gained ten pounds by eating and drinking like a frat boy; and then gained another ten pounds soon after by 'going on a diet' that consisted of eating my dessert *before* my dinner. As I got heavier and heavier my freshman year, I learned that a really easy way to forget that you've lost all control is to get blackout drunk and lose all control. So I did that for a few years, ashamed of my body, feeling hopeless."

Marta told me that for as long as she could remember, the idea of trying hard to look "perfect" (working out, eating healthily, wearing makeup) made her feel pathetic—so she just let it all go. "I felt like if I couldn't be perfect, there was no use trying," she said. She added that over the years she'd made a lot of progress in terms of how she felt about her body and her weight, but admitted that those childhood messages had been hard to shake. "Even now, at thirty-two, I have to consciously remind myself that I am more than my body," she said. "That if I can't fit into a pair of jeans, I still have a meaningful career and friends and family whom I love and who love me. I have to *remind* myself of these things. And that feels insane."

Unfortunately, the pressures to appear flawless are definitely not in our imagination. And neither is the fact that it's not the same for men. Hillary Clinton once remarked that during her 2008 presidential race, Barack Obama could just "roll out of bed and into a suit," while she spent hours prepping hair, makeup, and wardrobe before every appearance. When you're a woman on that size stage (I'd argue on any stage, for that matter), there's no room for error in how you look.

The examples are endless. Rihanna is photographed in baggy jeans one day and a sportswriter dedicates an entire blog post to how she "looks like she is wearing a sumo suit" and wondering whether she was "going to make being fat the hot new trend"? (Thankfully, the blowback was swift and he was summarily fired.) Jennifer Aniston once dared to eat a cheeseburger shortly before being photographed in a bikini and the entire Twittersphere was abuzz speculating whether she was "just gaining weight," or pregnant.

Just to add a little more fuel to the insecurity fire, these days we're not only supposed to look flawless, we're also supposed to pull off being thin and toned with straight white teeth, radiant skin, and glossy hair without looking like we're even trying. Seems growing up doesn't make us immune to the pressure of "effortless perfection" that plagues our girls. As a recent article by Amanda Hess in the *New York Times* points out, society now puts the onus on women to look within to overcome crises of beauty confidence, as if it's entirely self-generated and the unreasonable standards thrown at us from every direction don't exist. "The reality is that expectations for female appearance have never been higher," writes Hess. "It's just become taboo to admit that."

While most of us don't have to worry about our appearance being picked apart in the pages of *US Weekly*, we all feel body and beauty pressure in our own way. What's important here is to recognize how closely and incorrectly we've linked having a killer wardrobe, unblemished skin, and a toned booty with being perfect—and how false and fleeting the sense of control that gives us is.

A lovely woman named Evelyn told me a story about having to see her ex-husband and his new (much younger) wife at her daughter's wedding. She was so tied up in knots about it that she spent three months leading up to the event "perfecting" herself. She went on a strict diet to lose ten pounds, dyed her hair, and tried on countless dresses and shoes until she found the "perfect" combination. When the day of the wedding came, she looked spectacular—and still felt sad, jealous, and all the other emotions she was hoping to keep at bay. "Don't get me wrong," Evelyn said. "I felt like a million bucks, and that helped. But it wasn't a miracle cure—not by a long shot."

Obviously, I'm not suggesting we should all let ourselves go and start showing up for events or meetings looking like we don't give a crap. Appearance does matter, at least to a degree in terms of making a good impression. But having said that, there's a big difference between being appropriate and torturing ourselves in an attempt to look "perfect." If looking fabulous gives you a boost of confidence, by all means do it! Beauty is meant to be a joyful form of self-expression, and I'm the first person to admit that a bold red lipstick makes me feel on point. It's when we start obsessing and clutching on to flawlessness as a security blanket that we know we've tipped over into unhealthy territory.

Myth #2: Once Everything Is Perfect, I'll Be Happy

I once read that the amount of money a person needs to be happy is always 10 percent more than they have. That seems like a great analogy for how we chase the elusive carrot of perfection.

The thinking goes something like this: *If I look the right way, have the right job, land the right partner, everything will fall into place and I'll be happy.* I've fallen prey to this flawed logic myself. When I was younger, I thought if I worked out five times a week to have the "ideal" size 2 body like my sister's and went to Ivy League schools, I would meet the perfect guy who loved my brains and would support me unconditionally. We would have three perfect children and I'd become the president of the United States. I thought I could plan my life to be exactly as I dreamed, but only if I followed the script as perfectly as possible. I'm far from alone in this skewed perception.

To achieve our perfect ideal, we log our ten thousand steps a day, work out seven times a week, cut carbs out of our diets. We read endless articles, blogs, and books on how to advance in our careers, find work-life balance, attract the ideal partner. We go after the hot job or role in our community that everyone tells us we'd be perfect for. We have two point five kids, buy the perfect house, acquire all the right stuff.

And yet, are we happy?

The numbers say no. According to the National Institute of Mental Health, one out of every four women will experience severe depression in her lifetime. A seminal study done in 2009 at the University of Pennsylvania called "The Paradox of Declining Female Happiness" (how's that for telling?) showed that although women's lives have improved over the past thirty-five years in terms of increased opportunities, higher wages, and freedom from domestic drudgery via technological advancements, their happiness has declined. We *should* be happier, but we're not.

When we're chasing perfection, we can end up in jobs, relationships, and life situations we don't necessarily want to be in. We think that checking all the requisite boxes will lead to joy and fulfillment, but eventually we get to the bottom of the list and think, *Oh, shit . . . why am I not happy?*

Tonya is a talented illustrator who gets paid big bucks for her work. For more than twenty years, she's been regarded as one of the best in her business, with several prestigious awards to show for it. Her career provides her with lots of praise and admiration from others, not to mention good money. The only thing it doesn't bring her is joy.

Tonya doesn't hate her job; she's quick to point that out. But she doesn't love it, either. The spark went out of it for her a few years ago, and she's just going through the motions. She's got a decent amount of money saved, so that's not a major issue, but when I asked her why she didn't stop doing it and try something else that turned her on, she just sighed.

I know that sigh. I remember heaving it myself back when I was a young rising star at a fancy law firm, earning lots of praise and a big paycheck but hating every second of it. I've heard that sigh from many other women who feel stuck in roles in which they're "successful." I know it sounds funny to talk about being trapped by something we excel in. First world problems, right? But all problems demand we develop our bravery if they are ever to get solved.

One of the hallmarks of happiness is having close, meaningful connections with others. But keeping up a façade of having it all together keeps us isolated, because it keeps us from forging real, honest, deep relationships where we can fully be ourselves and feel accepted exactly as we are.

It's not that there's anything objectively wrong with our jobs, relationships, or lives—unless they are ones we didn't authentically choose; unless they are a reflection of everything we *believed* we were supposed to pursue rather than our real passions. After a lifetime of chasing other people's dreams (whether we're actually aware that's what we're doing or not), worrying about what others think, or following a prescribed formula for what we think our lives "should" look like, our own desires and goals get blurred. It's like driving a car with the navigation system yelling out dozens of different instructions all at the same time. Go right, go left, make a U-turn . . . eventually your own sense of direction gets drowned out.

We choose partners who fit the bill, even if we aren't genuinely in love or happy. (While this is speculation on my part, I don't think it's coincidental that the percentage of married women who report having affairs has risen 40 percent over the past twenty years.) We move into idyllic homes or lives—whatever form that takes for us—then feel disappointed that everything feels forced and plastic. Even with the people closest to us, we feel like we need to hide the truly ugly, messy, real stuff behind a glossy façade; then we wonder why our relationships feel hollow. We pursue opportunities or degrees that loved ones encourage us to do, believing that's the ticket to our happiness. Or, like a lot of women I met, we stay years too long in a career we don't love simply because we're good at it. Even when we wake up and realize that we are in the wrong career, or relationship, or life, the idea of making a change is terrifying, partly because we take it as a sign of failure and partly because it means we may have to go *way* outside our comfort zone to start over.

When I give talks at colleges, I often tell the story about how I spent so many years climbing the corporate ladder without ever questioning whether it was truly what I wanted. Once, after a speech I gave at Harvard, a young woman of color came running up to me as I was getting into a cab to say, "Everything you just said in your speech was ME." She told me about how she'd done everything she could to get to where she is pursuing a Ph.D. in early learning education, never asking herself if that was going to make her happy. She realized now that wasn't at all what she wanted to do, but she was doing it because it was simply the next credential she was tracked to earn.

Cindy is a stunning woman who literally looks like she stepped off the pages of a fitness magazine. She told me about how she'd finally reached the state of absolute physical perfection that she'd always wanted, but it ended up feeling empty. She wasn't any happier, her marriage wasn't any better, her teenage son's mental health issues were not any more under control. It seems that even if you do get to flawless, not much changes. No fireworks, no trophies, no guarantee of happiness—nothing but a vague sense of dissatisfaction and a feeling of *Is this it?*

We are trained to assume that if we connect all the perfect dots, it's going to bring us fulfillment. We don't even know how much of this in so ingrained in us. The thought is revolutionary when it hits us: Maybe "the perfect life" isn't really all that perfect after all.

Myth #3: If I'm Not Perfect, Everything Will Fall Apart

When flawlessness is the ideal, flaws by definition cannot be tolerated. It's not so much the mistakes we make that get to us; it's what we make them mean. In the mind of a perfectionist, a mistake is a sign of a personal flaw. The internal spin happens fast: It's not just that I rambled a little in a meeting;

it's that my colleagues will now forever think I'm stupid. It's not that I forgot to send in the permission slip for the class trip; it's that my kid's teacher—and probably my kid—now thinks I'm a shitty parent. It's not just that my date will be disappointed that I had to cancel on him at the last minute; now he'll never ask me out again and I'll die alone.

Lilly, an assistant to a publicist, spent an entire weekend in the throes of panic because she hadn't answered an email as soon as she should have, and she was sure her boss would be upset when she found out. "On Saturday I went to lunch with a girlfriend and spiraled all the way into, 'Maybe I should just forget working and go back for my master's . . .' I was so scared I was going to get fired, I came in at seven a.m. Monday morning and organized everything in sight so I could be beyond reproach."

I came across a recent study done by a professor at Auburn University which found that fewer women than men believe they meet their own standards in terms of family and work commitments. One expert commenting on the study added that women experience a lot of guilt as they try to juggle their work and home life. No disrespect meant here, but my immediate response when I read these shocking newsbreaks was, "Well . . . *duh.*"

I don't think the pressure to do everything perfectly shows up anywhere more profoundly than for working moms. Let's be serious: even when we have amazing 50/50 spouses or life partners, we are usually the ones who know what's in the diaper bag, or remember to grab the pacifier, or have the babysitter's numbers on speed dial. We've done a great job of internalizing the message that anything less than a perfect mom equals a bad mom.

I travel a lot for my work and feel unrelenting pressure and guilt about spending too much time apart from my kid. So I am constantly editing and reediting my schedule to minimize the time I'm away. When I'm in town, I'll get up at 5 a.m. to go to the gym so I'm done before my son gets up and I can sit with him while he eats breakfast and get him dressed for school. My husband is a great dad, but he doesn't have that same kind of guilt. If he has an early meeting and I'm not in town, he has no problem letting the babysitter do the breakfast and dressing routine. Even our bulldog, Stan, activates my mom guilt: when she's up and howling to go out at 7 a.m., I'll take her, even though I know that when I'm away, she'll happily snooze until 10 a.m. when Nihal is showered, shaved, and dressed.

Women are the ones who give away all of our "me" time to our partners and our children. But let's be brutally honest here: we often bring this on ourselves. Could our partners pack the diaper bag and make the kids' breakfast and make arrangements with the babysitter? Absolutely. Will they do it exactly the way we want them to? Probably not. But if we assume they won't do it 100 percent right, we figure we'll just do it our damn selves.

A national survey designed by the Families and Work Institute revealed that much of the time pressure women deal with is self-imposed because they have trouble delegating or letting go of control. Some have argued that women take on more of these parenting tasks because they are more nurturing by nature. But how much of what we're talking about here is really fundamental nurturing? When I think about nurturing, I think of tending to my son's physical and emotional well-being: caring for him when he spikes a fever, comforting him when his favorite stuffed froggy goes missing. It's our modern-day obsession with being the perfect mom—or what feminist sociologist Sharon Hayes dubbed "the ideology of intensive mothering"—not a nurturing instinct, that tells me I have to have every one of the necessary (and very best) school supplies on hand, feed him organic snacks, and teach him the alphabet before he turns twenty-one months old because we (okay, I) read somewhere that that's a sign of genius.

Dads, for the most part, don't feel that same pressure. They don't feel the same soul-crushing guilt if they don't nail the parenting minutia, because they never aimed for that perfection marker in the first place. I laugh every time I see the Pedigree Dentastix commercial featuring a young dad supervising his very messy toddler eating in the high chair. The child ends up with food all over his face, so the dad runs out of the room to get a wet towel to clean him up. By the time he gets back, the family dog has licked the baby's face clean. Dad pauses, assesses the situation, then shrugs and cheerfully responds, "That'll work."

Can you imagine how freeing it would feel to be like that?

The image of washing your kid's face with doggie slobber aside, I want to emphasize that giving up the expectation of perfection is *not* the same as being a bad parent or lowering your standards. It isn't the standards at all that we need to change, but our thinking about what it means if we do or don't reach them. It's great to want to feed your kid healthy meals. At the same time, he will not keel over from malnourishment if you feed him frozen chicken nuggets for dinner now and then. Punctuality and routine are good parenting practices. That being said, if you are unintentionally late to pick your kid up from day care because your rideshare was trapped behind a garbage truck, chances are you won't have done permanent psychological damage.

Being able to handle it all doesn't require perfection. It

demands bravery. It takes bravery to let go of control and delegate, to aim for 100 percent but be okay if you come in at 90, to make mistakes and own up to them without sliding into shame. It takes bravery to take care of yourself and say no when that voice in your head is telling you to sacrifice *everything* for your job and family (and your friend who calls for relationship advice six times a week . . . and your kid's PTA . . . and your neighbor who asked you to walk his dog while he's away . . .). It takes bravery to give yourself a break and refuse to let guilt dictate your daily life, and to model self-compassion for your kids by letting them see it's okay to screw up.

It takes bravery to retire our perfect girl and trade her in for the new model of brave woman. But it's worth it.

Myth #4: Perfection Is the Same as Excellence

It's easy to tell ourselves that we're aiming to be perfect because we have high standards and want to excel. What could be wrong with that? But our perfect girl training has muddied the waters here. The truth is we can be excellent *without* being perfect; they aren't one and the same.

The difference between excellence and perfection is like the difference between love and obsession. One is liberating, the other unhealthy. Perfection is an all-or-nothing game; you either succeed or fail, period. There are no small victories, no "A" for effort. If you're a perfection seeker and you fail at anything, it can really take you out.

When you are pursuing excellence, on the other hand, you don't let failure break you, because it's not a win or lose kind of game. Excellence is a way of being, not a target you hit or miss. It allows you to take pride in the effort you put in regardless of the outcome. I'll be the first one to tell you that it's great to have high personal standards. You *should* prepare well and strive to do your best in that interview, meeting, event, speech, game, or project—personal or professional. There's nothing wrong with having a healthy desire to excel, even to win. What's *not* okay is setting impossible goals and expectations or beating yourself up if you don't get the ideal results.

You know you're crossing the line from the pursuit of excellence into perfectionism when you feel like nothing is ever enough. A big clue is if you don't know when to celebrate. I still have to watch myself on this one. People will say, "Wow, Reshma, you've accomplished a lot," and immediately a needling little voice in my head says, *Not really.* That's the ghost of perfectionism talking, and it sucks all the joy right out of the experience. But if you chase excellence instead of perfection, you get to actually feel proud of your achievements. These days, I'm working on taking moments to celebrate when I accomplish something. I'll turn up my girl Beyoncé really loud and dance around my living room, get one of those decadently good chocolate chip cookies from my favorite bakery, or even tweet a little congratulatory note to myself.

Perfection can really ruin a good thing. Instead of allowing us to see everything we did right, it demands that we hyperfocus on the one thing that wasn't 100 percent. For example, my TED talk has had over almost four million views; countless women have emailed to tell me how much it moved them, and *Fortune* magazine even called it one of the most inspiring speeches of 2016. But you know what I saw when I watched it? Overly curled hair and makeup that looks ridiculously vamped up. There I was making an impact on the lives of millions of girls and women, and all I could think was, *Why didn't anyone tell me I looked like I was going clubbing instead of getting onstage to give a speech in front of millions of people?*

When my friend Tiffany Dufu published her amazing book, *Drop the Ball*, it received glowing reviews and was hailed by Gloria Steinem as "important, path-breaking, intimate and brave." Instead of reveling in this incredible praise, she became fixated on a couple of negative Amazon reviews (even though they were far outnumbered by positive ones). "You'd have thought my world was falling apart every time anyone wrote something critical," she said. Another case of perfectionism robbing us of pride in excellence.

It's become a bit of a cliché to call yourself a perfectionist in a job interview, thinking it implies a strong work ethic and high attention to detail. The irony is that perfectionism actually *impedes* excellence. It causes us to overthink, overrevise, overanalyze: too much perfecting, not enough doing.

You might be thinking, *Sure, some imperfection is fine in some jobs, but we all want our trusted professionals, like doctors or lawyers, to be perfectionists, right?* But the research makes a compelling case for why that thinking is upside down. For example, a 2010 study of twelve hundred college professors found that those who strive for perfection are less likely to get published or receive citations. Research confirms that the most successful people in any given field are *less* likely to be perfectionistic, because the anxiety about making mistakes gets in your way, explained psychologist Thomas Greenspan in a *New York* magazine article. "Waiting for the surgeon to be absolutely sure the correct decision is being made could allow me to bleed to death."

Myth #5: Failure Is Not an Option

If failure isn't an option, then neither is taking risks. That, right there, is how perfection strangles bravery.

The fear of failure is so huge. We're afraid that if we try something outside our comfort zone and fall short, we'll look foolish and forever be identified with our failure. We're afraid it will be proof that we'll never meet our expectations of ourselves—or the expectations of others. We will end up disgraced, ashamed, emotionally and professionally decimated. What if it breaks us and we can't pick ourselves back up?

When I lost my congressional race, I thought I was done, washed up for good, my dream to be a public servant on a national scale dead in its tracks. I woke up the morning after in the hotel room my staff had (rather optimistically) decorated with congratulatory balloons and congratulatory notes stuck everywhere on Post-its, feeling sick to my stomach. I'd let down all the people who had invested in and supported me, my voters, my friends, my family. As a candidate, I was sure my career was in ruins; as a human, I felt utterly and sickeningly like garbage.

It took me a few months of nursing my wounds before I was ready to pick up my head. Once I did, I discovered a new dream that has allowed me to serve and make a difference in exactly the way I can now see that I was meant to. I'd always thought my calling was to be on Capitol Hill, but I found that if I wanted to innovate and make a real difference, my path would be through creating a movement of girl coders who will grow up to solve our nation's and our world's most pressing problems. And here's the thing: I never would have learned that if I hadn't tried something and failed. If I had never run for office, I never would have visited classrooms on the campaign trail and seen the gender divide in schools and the potential talent our economy was missing out on. I never would have had the idea for Girls Who Code and I never would have had the privilege to help tens of thousands of girls around the country believe that they can do anything. Nor would I have cultivated the rock-solid belief that *I* can do anything.

In start-up world, failure is celebrated as a necessary part of innovation, and the entrepreneurial "fail early and often" mentality is beginning to spread. These days, we're seeing a lot of momentum to destigmatize failure both in education and in the world of business, and I love it. Smith College, for example, recently launched a program called "Failing Well" to teach high-achieving students how to deal with and even embrace setbacks, and Stanford, Harvard, Penn, and others have followed suit with similar initiatives. At the NYC-based media start-up theSkimm, founders Danielle Weisberg and Carly Zakin instituted a "Fail So Hard" hat ritual in which they pass around a hard hat at staff meetings for anyone who tried something new and failed that week to proudly wear while sharing their story.

I'm here to tell you that failing IS an option. I didn't just fail when I lost my race for the US Congress, I also did it again in 2013, in an unsuccessful bid for the office of public advocate of New York City. I failed last month when I spaced and forgot my niece's birthday, and again this morning when I put on my son's diaper and he peed on me. By failing, I learned how to embrace imperfection. I'm not afraid of either anymore. In the words of Hillary Clinton, I'd rather be "caught trying" than not at all.

Myth #6: I Need to Be Perfect to Get Ahead

Sadly, it is still true that women need to work twice as hard to earn the same respect as men in their work. Being the ultimate overachievers, most of us take that to mean that to succeed we need to not just be excellent—we need to be perfect.

The problem here is that perfection *doesn't* get us ahead. In fact, it sabotages us in more ways than we even realize.

A study released in 2015 from LeanIn.org and McKinsey & Co shows that women don't step up to positions of senior leadership not because of family obligations, but because they don't want the stress and pressure that comes along with that level of responsibility. As the *Wall Street Journal* reported in a summary of this study, "The path to senior positions is disproportionately stressful for women." I believe this is true, but I think this disproportionate stress arises in part because women think they need to do the job perfectly.

How many career opportunities have we passed up because we were afraid of being rejected or failing? How many times have we begged off an assignment or promotion saying, "I'm just not good at that"? No question that the glass ceiling and double bind are factors in women's advancement, but I believe our perfect-girl hardwiring is also a significant part of the reason women are underrepresented in leadership positions in the corporate world, in government, and elsewhere. Women don't run for office because they believe they won't fare as well as men, even though the research proves that's not at all the case. It's the fear of exposing our less-than-perfect selves or the belief that we don't have the ideal leadership skills that interferes, not capability.

I have worked with many men in law, in finance, and now in the tech industry, and one trait they all seem to have in common is a willingness to step up to take on a challenge—regardless of whether or not they're ultraprepared for it. If I ask my team at Girls Who Code who wants to spearhead a new business opportunity, without fail the dudes around the table will immediately step up—even the ones who've never done anything in that area before. Like the time my VP of finance, for example, eagerly volunteered to take over Human Resources even though he had zero prior HR experience and the organization was looking to grow by 300 percent over the next year. If I ask one of my female employees to head up a big project in new and unfamiliar territory, however, more often than not she'll question whether she's qualified to take the lead or ask if she can sleep on it (which most of the time comes back with a no).

I've seen countless men launch entire businesses without worrying about having the relevant training or expertise. Jack Dorsey, a cofounder of Twitter, started Square because he was curious about finding a way to make payments easier, not because he was knowledgeable about mobile payment. He had no experience building a financial services company, but that didn't stand in his way. Three tech dudes in their twenties founded the cool and successful beauty product app Hush when they realized—almost by accident—that makeup was the top seller on their bargain-driven site. Instead of saying, "We're guys . . . we don't know anything about makeup," they went out and put together a staff that was 60 percent women to steer them in the right direction.

This is in stark contrast to Tina, the smart, talented woman who cuts my hair. Tina wants to open her own salon, but because she doesn't know how to build a website or start a company, she's resigned herself to staying where she is. So much of this is tied into the "effortless perfection" ideal we've been taught as girls. As Rachel Simmons points out, when you believe you're supposed to make it all look easy, and pretend like you've got a handle on everything, you lose out on building a very important skill: admitting you need help. Instead of asking for help with her idea, Tina talked herself out of it. At some time or another, most of us have done the same.

The perfection ideal also hits us squarely in the paycheck. There has been a lot of talk about why there is a persistent wage gap between men and women. Is the gender and structural discrimination women face an insurmountable barrier? Are women simply picking industries that pay less? Or is it the pressure we put on ourselves to do the job perfectly that makes us opt out of high-paying opportunities? There's also the negotiation factor to consider when we think about money we may be leaving on the table. It's difficult to press for more when you're worried about seeming pushy.

This fear lurks in the majority of women, no matter how accomplished or powerful. When Academy Award–winning actress Jennifer Lawrence discovered that she earned significantly less than her male costars on the blockbuster hit *American Hustle*, she blamed herself for not having pressed for her fair share because she'd been worried about how she would be perceived. "I would be lying if I didn't say there was an element of wanting to be liked that influenced my decision to close the deal without a real fight," she wrote in the feminist newsletter *Lenny*. "I didn't want to seem 'difficult' or 'spoiled.' At the time, that seemed like a fine idea, until I saw the payroll on the Internet and realized every man I was working with definitely didn't worry about being 'difficult' or 'spoiled.'" That's exactly why we need to cultivate the courage to demand and earn the money we deserve.

The only thing Perfect Girl 3.0 can tolerate less than making mistakes is getting negative feedback. Nora works at the front desk of a hotel, where she's given quarterly performance reviews. Even if 90 percent of her review is positive, she zooms right in on the 10 percent her boss says needs improvement. Even though it's meant to show how and when she can better serve the hotel guests, all she hears is how she's screwed up and disappointed her boss. "I take it well up front, but I die inside," she said. "It eats me alive for days."

Stand up straight . . . fix your hair . . . don't mumble. But wait. If we're used to getting this kind of needling input throughout our young lives, why do we then fall apart later in life when we get less-than-glowing feedback? Why didn't that chorus of criticisms translate into grit? Likely because we're getting that input when we're too young to hear it as anything but disapproval. We don't see it as constructive advice from a loving parent trying to teach us how to present ourselves, but as disapproval. So naturally, later on, we experience the smallest criticisms as an indictment of our character.

This inability to tolerate negative feedback holds us back professionally, because it prevents us from taking in *constructive* feedback that could actually help us improve. I've had more than one guy tell me they avoid giving their female coworkers criticism—no matter how helpful feedback might be for the outcome of a project or situation—because they're afraid it will "make them cry." And unfortunately, sometimes they're right. If that's not a snapshot of perfection sabotaging us, I don't know what is.

Just like we're smart enough to know intellectually that perfection holds us back in all these ways and more, we're also wise enough to understand that just being aware of these myths doesn't mean the decades of training that went into them disappear overnight. As great as it would be to read a book and magically be free from the shackles of perfectionism, it doesn't work that way. The real key to breaking free is by retraining yourself to embrace bravery, which you'll learn how to do in Part Three. Then, and only then, does Perfect Girl 3.0 fade into the shadows, making way for the bold, confident woman to emerge.

The Truth about Perfection

Beyond all the myths about perfection lies one essential truth:
Perfect is boring.

We hold up the notion of "perfect" as the ultimate goal. No mistakes, no flaws, no rough edges. But the reality is that it's the messy, unfinished edges that make us interesting and our lives rich. Embracing our imperfection creates joy. Plus, if you're already perfect, where's the fun in learning or striving? I've always loved the stories about President Obama playing basketball. He wasn't great at it; he wasn't even technically that good. But he loved it, and so he practiced and practiced—and he got better at both getting the ball through the net, and at being okay with being less than perfect. Training a new part of his brain felt satisfying—and that quality was part of what made him a great leader.

The most interesting people I know have flaws and quirks that make them uniquely amazing. My friend Natalie is chronically late—but blows in every time with a thrilling story about where she's just come from. Daaruk leaves a mess all over our apartment whenever he comes to New York and stays with us—but has one of the most fascinating creative minds I've ever seen. Adita has absolutely no filter and will say whatever pops into her head; her observations may sting sometimes, but they are usually spot-on and helpful critiques. As for me, I know I love to be right and can be a little (okay, a lot) forceful about that, but that's what makes me such a stubborn champion for my ideals.

If you think about it, it's actually kind of funny that we even strive to be perfect in the first place, given how unfulfilling it is if and when you get there.

Bravery, on the other hand, is a pursuit that adds to your life everything perfection once threatened to take away: authentic joy; a sense of genuine accomplishment; ownership of your fears and the grit to face them down; an openness to new adventures and possibilities; acceptance of all the mistakes, gaffes, flubs, and flaws that make you interesting, and that make your life uniquely *yours*.

Part Two

Brave Is the New Black

4

Redefining Bravery

As I write this, a watershed moment for women and bravery is playing out on the national stage. It began, of course, in the fall of 2017, when we witnessed just how awesome female bravery can be.

When the *New York Times* published a blistering picture of Hollywood titan Harvey Weinstein revealing decades of alleged sexual harassment, it unleashed a flood of personal stories. It felt like every day I'd get a fresh "Breaking News" alert on my phone about another powerful dude in entertainment, sports, academia, media, or politics who had used his status to harass, harm, and intimidate women into silence. Slowly at first, and then with shocking volume and speed, women joined the thunderous chorus of the #MeToo movement and freed themselves from years of shame. They came out from behind the fear and said: *No more.* No more silencing our voices. No more playing nice. No more trading in our self-worth or accepting patronizing bullshit and abuse because "that's just how it is." The results were historic, as the previously untouchable careers and reputations of these men instantaneously were reduced to smoldering ashes.

The #MeToo movement gave countless women their voices back, but it also showed the world what can happen when women band together and choose bravery. But it also gave us a different way to talk about bravery: why it matters, who has it (um, everyone), and, most of all, how we define what it means to be brave.

As of the writing of this book, we don't yet know if this movement will inspire the long-term, systemic changes in the lopsided power dynamic we desperately need. But the trends we are seeing give me real hope. I watched with pride as Serena Williams broke the unspoken genteel rules of her sport and dared to take an emotional and defiant stand at the U.S Open against the obvious bias levied at her, in an effort to clear her name and speak out for all female tennis players. I sat glued to the television with awe watching a terrified but determined Dr. Christine Blasey Ford testify before the Senate about her assault at the hands of Supreme Court Justice Brett Kavanaugh. This is how women will change the world, one brave voice at a time.

We are seeing more and more women displaying bravery in so many ways, including daring to defy entrenched stereotypes, claiming our voices and speaking out against injustice, shattering glass ceilings, and much more. It's time to redefine courage as a trait attainable by anyone and everyone, regardless of gender or biology.

Is Bravery a Male Trait?

Spoiler alert: No!

One of the most memorable responses I got to my TED talk about bravery was from a guy who posted a comment on the website Armed and Dangerous (its tagline: Sex, Software, Politics, and Firearms. Life's Simple Pleasures . . .) arguing that women are less brave because of our ovaries. Yes, you read that right: our ovaries.

He claimed that women are naturally more cautious and fearful because evolution has wired us that way. According to him, "women have only a limited number of ovulations in their lifetime and, in the EAA (environment of ancestral adaptation), pregnancy was a serious risk of death. Contrast this with men, who have an effectively unlimited supply of sperm—any individual male is far less critical to a human group's reproductive success than any individual female. Do the game theory. It would be crazy if women weren't *instinctively* far more risk-averse than men."

Well, listen up, sir: my ovaries have no say in how brave I choose to be. His reasoning may sound logical and elicit nods of approval from his male cronies, but his science is faulty at best. These kinds of arguments are sadly commonplace and need to be dismantled, *now*.

Bravery is not innate. Males are not biologically ordained to be the braver sex, and testosterone isn't the singular almighty ticket to courage. Unfortunately, this "men are hardwired to be braver" argument has been made many times in different shades. I'm sure you've heard any number of these variations: Our brains are wired differently when it comes to risk. Men are braver because they have more testosterone, or because they have been prehistorically programmed to woo reproductive partners with their bold prowess. I'm calling bullshit on all of it.

The evolutionary argument essentially comes down to reproductive success, or survival of the fittest. But this theory that male bravery is a trait that will enable the species to continue is also in need of a refresh. Today the whole Me Tarzan/You Jane notion of the big, burly caveman who fearlessly hunts down giant mastodons while his barefoot and pregnant wife hangs safely back at the cave ground nurturing the home and hearth is, to say the least, outdated. It may have taken millions of years, but we've evolved *way* past the days of a woman's job being restricted to gathering berries, or baking pies, or mixing a dry martini and acting as pleasant ornamentation.

Bravery in today's world is far more than just physical prowess, and we see hundreds of examples all around us of girls and women being brave as hell in myriad ways. From transgender soldier Chelsea Manning who exposed classified information about government corruption, to Australian senator Larissa Waters who boldly laid claim to working moms' rights and breastfed her daughter on the floor of Parliament, to the hundreds of women who risked their livelihood and reputations to blow the whistle on sexual assault at the hands of powerful men, we've amassed plenty of proof that the scope and definition of bravery has evolved mightily.

All this ends up being good news for us as women, because while we can't change biology, we sure as hell can change our environment—or at least how we respond to it. Just like we learned to be perfect girls, we teach ourselves how to be brave women.

A New View of Bravery

In 2013, I had two major life events. I lost my race for public advocate and I suffered my third miscarriage a few months later. I was a mess. All these bad things were happening to me and I didn't feel like I could stop them.

Not long after, my husband dragged me on a trip to New Zealand for our friend Jun's wedding. Jun is a little bit of an adventure nut, so the entire trip was centered on getting his wedding party to do semidangerous things. One of the activities on the agenda was bungee jumping. Now, I am terrified of heights. As in, I want to throw up when I am at the top of a building, so you can understand why I really didn't want to hurl my body off a bridge suspended only by an elastic band around my ankle. At the same time, my life felt out of control, and somehow I sensed that letting go of my fear of heights and going for it would allow me to let go of the lingering frustration and sadness I'd been carrying around, too.

So I jumped. Yes, in a tandem with my husband and with my eyes squeezed shut the whole time while I prayed to every Hindu god I knew, but I jumped. It was terrifying, but I'd be lying if I didn't say that flying through the air wasn't also thrilling and liberating. After that trip, I came back to the States, restarted my career, and tried yet again to have a baby—both of which worked out better than I ever dreamed.

Which of these acts was the bravest? If you go by the traditional (a.k.a. male) definition of brave, you'd probably say the bungee jump. But true bravery is more than being a daredevil. I consider *all three* of these choices—the jump, the career reboot after a humiliating loss, the pregnancy attempt after three devastating miscarriages—personal acts of bravery. Bravery takes so many different forms, and they're all important and valuable. *All bravery matters* because bravery feeds on itself. We build our bravery muscles one act at a time, big or small. This is what I mean when I say it's time for us to redefine bravery, on our terms.

In a World Full of Princesses, Dare to Be a Hot Dog

So how do I define bravery?

Bravery is my friend Carla who walked away from a massively successful company she'd built because her relationship with her cofounder had grown toxic. It took her a few years to work up the courage to leave because she'd given so much of herself to building the business and had banked so much on its success and didn't know who she would be if she was no longer a part of it.

Bravery is Sharon who gave up a comfortable twenty-five-year marriage and easy life because she knew deep down that she was gay and would regret it the rest of her life if she didn't follow her heart. It's my son's babysitter Audrey who battled and survived breast cancer. It's every woman who chose a life path or partner her family doesn't approve of, who had a baby on her own, or honored her inner voice that said motherhood *wasn't* the path for her. It's every woman who went back to school or to work after her kids were born, and every woman who chose not to. It's any woman who had the guts to shatter the illusion that she has it all together and ask for help.

Bravery is every woman who has spoken out against mistreatment, even if it meant risking her career or reputation. It's every woman who let herself off the hook for making a mistake, who gives herself a pass for feeding her kids pizza every once in a while instead of a home-cooked meal, who, when she knows she's wrong, says "I'm sorry" without being defensive or shifting blame.

It's brave to rock who you are, loud and proud and without apologies. We see examples of this all around us, and not only in the expected places. Not long ago, a photo of a five-year-old girl named Ainsley from North Carolina went viral after she showed up for "Princess Week" at her dance class dressed not as Cinderella or one of the sisters from *Frozen*—but as a hot dog. Her dance teacher was so wowed by Ainsley's gutsy choice that she posted a picture, and the Internet went nuts. Across the Twittersphere, people cheered for this little girl who unknowingly inspired every one of us who dream of letting our own freak flag fly. My favorite tweet: *In a world full of princesses, dare to be a hot dog.*

It just might be that today's youngest generation of girls could teach us a thing or two about bravery. My friend Valerie has a daughter who has known she was transgender from the time she was seven years old. Valerie helped her transition at that young age from James to Jasmine, and when Jasmine started a new school the following year, no one knew. She kept her birth identity a secret, unsure of whether she would be made fun of—or worse. In one of the most moving acts of bravery I can imagine, when her class was learning about gender identity, little Jasmine came out and told her classmates her secret. For a few short moments, they sat in surprised silence before gathering around to give Jasmine hugs of support and tell her they were proud to be her friend.

Bravery is taking an unpopular stand when everyone expects you to go along with the program—and then refusing to back down. In January 2017, a few days after President Trump was inaugurated, I received a phone call from Ivanka Trump's office inviting me to the White House to discuss a computer science education initiative she was spearheading. Then, a few days later, the president signed the executive order blocking the entry of citizens from seven predominantly Muslim countries. As the daughter of refugees myself I felt both sickened and a strong obligation to stand up for the many Muslim girls who participate in Girls Who Code. I declined Ms. Trump's invitation to partner with this administration.

Later that year, many big-name tech leaders gathered at an event in Detroit to celebrate the Education Department's commitment of $200 million for computer science education. Many were and still are my friends and industry colleagues. I did not attend, again feeling I had to take a stand against an administration that has inflicted such harm through its bigotry.

I felt so strongly about this that I decided to double-down

and agreed to write an op-ed for the *New York Times* explaining my position. I'll level with you: I was terrified the morning it was due to come out. I believed so deeply in what I was saying, and at the same time knew that some people in the tech industry would be very pissed off. It's very hard to stand up to powerful people, and I was acutely aware of the fact that there could be real fallout. I knew I could lose funding, because I called out some of Girls Who Code's biggest supporters, mostly tech giants and leaders who would not appreciate having their moral courage called into question. But I knew I had to brave my fear and do what I thought was right. I would rather have stood up to this issue than be silent in the face of a bully just because I was beholden to my funders.

Amazingly, the backlash I was braced for never came. Instead, donations for small amounts poured in from all over the country, along with notes of gratitude and support. Teachers who longed to see more diversity wrote to cheer me on, moms wrote to say "thank you" for my stance because, as one said, "There are things that should never be normalized." My point here isn't that I should be congratulated; it's that risky acts— like taking an unpopular stand— might be scary, but they often end up being the ones that are most appreciated and celebrated.

It takes guts to be the first one to do something, to break new ground. Take the brave women who called out Bill Cosby and came forward with their allegations against Bill O'Reilly, Roger Ailes, then presidential candidate Donald Trump, investors in Silicon Valley, and many others, even knowing there was a strong likelihood that no one would believe their stories. This was before the Harvey Weinstein floodgates opened, unleashing the groundswell that became the #MeToo movement—which makes what these women did even braver. Their stories were largely discounted, their reputations were irreversibly smeared, and they were subjected to vicious threats and hateful attacks in the media, and yet, they refused to back down.

For a short while, it looked like all their pain was for nothing. But as we now know, it was anything but. Though they had no way of knowing it at the time, these women opened a tiny crack in the fault line, which grew into one of the biggest earthquakes in our modern social history. Without them, who knows if #MeToo ever would have happened? One thing I know for sure is that bravery is contagious, and when even one lone woman stands up, it inspires so many others to do the same.

Those are the big, public forms of bravery. Yet the quiet ones we tackle in our private moments are just as valuable. One of my Girls Who Code alums, Valentina, decided to grow out her natural curly hair in her junior year of high school. This may seem like an insignificant decision, but at her school, this just wasn't done; the standard of beauty was sleek, flattened hair. Did some kids make rude comments? Yes. But after so many girls told her privately that they wished they had the guts to do the same thing, Valentina decided to start a club at her school called Know Your Roots. "Society makes us feel like we need to straighten our hair just to fit in," she said. "I didn't know how many other girls felt insecure and struggle with feeling beautiful with their hair just as it is."

Bravery isn't always about doing the biggest, boldest, baddest thing. Sometimes it's braver to give yourself permission to be true to yourself by *not* doing something that is expected of you. When my son was born, for example, I assumed I would breastfeed him for as long as possible. That's what every book (and nurse in the hospital . . . and other mom I met . . .) told me I was supposed to do, and of course I wanted the very best for him, so I committed to it. I was going to be the best mom ever, damn it!

Once I went back to work, things got complicated. I found myself frantically searching every three hours for a private bathroom to pump, spilling breast milk down my blouse in tiny, smelly airplane bathrooms, and setting my alarm for 5 a.m. to get in a feeding before leaving for work. I was frustrated, exhausted, and miserable—not to mention pissed as hell at my husband for not having to deal with breastfeeding. Where was the joy of new motherhood I'd been promised? I turned to my friend Esther Perel, the renowned psychotherapist and relationship expert, for help. When I told her what was going on, she looked at me, and said plainly, "Just stop breastfeeding."

Bam! Her words hit me like a ton of bricks. I had literally *never even considered* that it was an option not to breastfeed. I stopped, and within days, I fell in love with being a mother. Finally, I could be the parent I wanted to be for my child, instead of continuing on as a pumping, crying, frustrated mess.

For every woman like the above-mentioned Sharon who bravely left a marriage, there's another woman who bravely chose to stay. For many years, it was believed that the bravest choice a woman can make when her spouse cheats is to leave and strike out on her own, not least because of the shame attached with getting a divorce. However, as Esther points out in her new book called *The State of Affairs: Rethinking Infidelity*, it isn't divorce that carries the stigma anymore. These days, choosing to *stay* if a partner has been unfaithful is looked down upon far more. And yet, for some, it may be the right choice. "Women have all kinds of reasons why they decide this one experience won't be the deciding factor in a decades-long relationship, and they should be able to do that without the fear of judgment of everyone around them," she says.

It's brave to respect yourself enough to say no to something you don't want to do, especially if it means disappointing a friend or loved one. It's nuts how hard this can be sometimes, isn't it? Our perfect-girl training that urges us to be helpful and accommodating at all costs is damn hard to shake. How many times have you agreed to go to a party, sit on a committee or board, volunteer at your kid's school, lend a family member money, or do a big favor for a friend that deep down you really didn't want to do? It takes guts to be able to say, "I'm sorry but I just don't have the time to take that on right now," and even more guts to say, "Thank you, but no," without the apology or excuse (I'm still working on that one . . .).

When you've got the "perfection or bust" conditioning, it's brave to put yourself out there and do something when you're not sure you'll succeed. Sue Lin worked for months on a treatment for a new comedy show and was terrified to send the pitch email to the content buyer at Netflix for fear she'd fall to pieces if it were rejected. But she prayed on it and hit send anyway. Marissa was terrified to start dating again after her divorce, but she wrote up a profile and joined an online dating site anyway. She knew, as we all do, that there are no guarantees, but she also knew that she was 100 percent more likely to meet someone by putting herself out there than by staying home binge watching *Downton Abbey*.

Bottom line here is that we need to recast bravery as far more than one-dimensional. It's broad, complex, and context-specific—that is, a person may be bold in one area but not another. You can be bold and fierce in your entrepreneurial spirit but skittish in dating, or perfectly comfortable investing in the stock market but wouldn't in a million years skydive. I've stood and given speeches in front of tens of thousands of people, but the thought of getting up to do karaoke at a friend's birthday party scares the hell out of me.

It's also deeply personal. For some, rappelling off a cliff is the bravest thing imaginable; for others, it's giving a speech in front of twenty people. Soldiers who fight on the battlefield are brave; so are the women who fight for the right to birth control and reproductive choice. First responders who step up to save lives are brave; so are the women who risk their livelihood to speak up about sexual assault at the hands of powerful men. Senator John McCain was brave in September 2017 when he crossed party lines to stand up for what he believes; so was Shonda Rhimes when she made interracial couples the norm on her groundbreaking hit television shows.

It's all bravery, and it all matters.

Brave like Women

It's no coincidence that our society has adopted the phrase "she's got balls" as a perverse compliment for when a woman does something bold or gutsy. The implication, of course, is that men's testicles are their seat of bravery and power. Well, just like we don't need to be like men to be brave, we definitely don't need to be like men to succeed. This is old, tired thinking that I'm so over.

It's not as though acting like a dude really gets us anywhere anyway. At work, even when women adopt the same career advancement strategies, they still get lower pay. We've heard again and again about the double bind we face: If we aren't nurturing, warm, and kind, we aren't liked—but we get shut out of leadership positions if we are. We're damned if we're confident, outspoken, and gutsy, and doomed if we aren't. Study after study shows that when women display stereotypically "masculine" traits such as toughness or nonverbal dominance (i.e., staring someone in the eye when speaking), they can come up against intense backlash. The receptivity to women displaying assertive behavior in the workplace just isn't there. I want to add, "For now." I am confident that if we reach back and start rewiring kids early, cutting out the gendered behaviors at the pass, we start changing this generationally.

But what about us here and now? To escape this double bind, we need to become brave not like men, but *brave like women*. We need to say, fuck the traditional rules and definitions, and do it our way, because we know that our contributions are just as valuable—if not more so. It's time to play to our strengths instead of hiding them, no matter how "masculine" or "feminine" we think they are. Women are more emotional than men? Awesome. I say that's an asset, not a liability, and the research backs that up. As just one of many examples, a report from PriceWaterhouseCooper and the Crowdfunding Center showed that women are 32 percent more successful at generating funds via crowdfunding than men. Why? Because they use more emotional and inclusive language in their pitches, which investors found more appealing than the clichéd sports and war metaphors and the typical dry business language.

It's the same with women and risk-taking. Yes, women are generally more risk averse than men. But where you might say timid, I say intelligently cautious and thoughtful. There's a reason why so many speculated that the economic crisis would never have happened if it were Lehman Sisters running the show.

We have spent so much time trying to figure out how to get into the game following the rules written by men. That makes about as much sense to me as trying to explore uncharted territory by following somebody else's path. We can't become unique by copying someone else's formula any more than we can become successful by striving for someone else's definition of success. And really, what's the point of succeeding by someone else's rules anyway?

We need to change our approach and do things authentically. Being brave like women is about making choices based on what we want and what makes us happy, not what others expect or want for us. If being a senator or a Fortune 500 CEO are your true goals, awesome! But they don't have to be. Just as there is no one "right" way to be brave, there is no one universal definition of success.

Look, we know the biases against women exist in the workplace, in politics, and elsewhere. There are real structural challenges against women. There's no denying that. Of the five hundred thousand elected officials in this country, 79 percent are still white men. Does that mean that if you're a brown-skinned woman you shouldn't run for office? Of course not. It means you should accept the challenges, recognize you might fail, and *do it anyway*.

I'm not telling you to just try harder to achieve your goals. What I am telling you is not to let fear stop you from going after them. I'm telling you not to give up before you try. If you succeed, the success will be even sweeter because it was fueled by courage and by genuine passion. If you don't, you may be disappointed but you will still feel proud, because it will be what Carol Dweck calls an "honest failure."

We've come a long way, but the reality is that it will still be a while before we see big changes in the gender equality landscape. That's the bad news. The good news is that how we respond and act in the face of these obstacles is up to us. I believe we need to stop trying to wrestle for power, respect, and opportunities from others and instead bravely make them for ourselves.

Don't misunderstand me: I think we need to keep pushing as hard as we can for cultural change. It's not okay for our girls to grow up in a world that tells them they have to starve themselves to meet some unrealistic standard of beauty, or that getting a degree in computer programming or speaking their minds is the exclusive domain of boys. We need to create a better world for them and for ourselves, and I believe we do this by defining bravery on our own terms one cause, one goal, one failure, one hot dog in a world of princesses at a time. We do it by cultivating the bravery that lives inside each and every one of us.

5

Why Be Brave?

If you think about it, pretty much everything worth doing in life requires bravery. Bravery is why we try that twentieth cartwheel that we triumphantly nail after falling nineteen times. It's what sends us off to college or far from home where we don't know anyone, what encourages us to follow a passion into our first job. Bravery enables us to start a business, change careers, or ask for the salary we deserve. It allows us to be vulnerable enough to ask for help and helps us muster the strength to forgive someone who hurt us. It inspires us to be generous and support other women without fearing that it diminishes us. As Winston Churchill once said, "Courage is the first of human virtues because it makes all others possible."

Bravery makes falling in love possible. It takes courage to allow someone to see the real you, flaws and all, and to accept someone else who is equally imperfect. As Esther Perel told me, bravery allows us to be vulnerable and reciprocal, which in turn makes relationships robust. "People sometimes do the wrong things or hurt each other's feelings . . . being able to speak up about it or say 'I fucked up, I'm sorry' takes bravery," she says. "Bravery is the ability to see yourself as flawed and own it without plunging instantly into shame. It's also the ability to experience joy for the great things that happen to the other person, even if they have nothing to do with you."

Bravery transforms *all* our relationships from glossy and shellacked to honest, raw, and real. How often are we honest—truly honest—with our friends? Only by building your bravery muscles, does the veneer get melted and true heart-to-heart connections are forged. I have a crew of seven girlfriends from law school. Life got busy and we see each other now only once or twice a year, but when we do, it's like no time passed. We talk about the deeper stuff that's going on—the miscarriages, the bumps in our marriages, the fears we carry that no one else ever sees. It takes courage to open up like that to other human beings, but it's such a privilege to have this kind of safe space to be fully open and real.

Bravery makes us better parents. When we let go of the unrealistic expectations for ourselves, we then naturally ease up on our kids. When we stop obsessing about our kids' grades or college essays, we help them see the joy in learning. We show them by example how to pursue excellence without making it about perfection, and that the world won't end if they screw up or fail. It's brave to allow your kid to be exactly who they are and do what they love, *even if you don't agree with their choices.* They're happier and healthier for it, though, and so are you.

This may sound a little cheesy, but bravery helps us turn our dreams into reality. I don't care if your dream is to be in the C-suite, quit your job and start a business, be a hip-hop dancer, come out to your family, work at an animal sanctuary, run a marathon, go back to school, publish a novel, get married and have children, or make your mark on the world through activism—bravery will help get you from here to there.

Forget cultivating the perfectly polished exterior; that's just a flimsy façade that can come toppling down at any minute.

When we build our bravery muscles, we're safe for real because we know we can handle whatever comes our way. Bravery doesn't guarantee that everything will work out, just that we'll be okay if it doesn't. No matter what demons we face, bravery allows us to stand strong and *keep going*. Bravery—not perfection—is the only true armor there is.

Bravery keeps us afloat when we might otherwise sink. As we all know, shit happens in life that we can't control. We lose jobs, face health crises, lose loved ones—these are hard realities we can't avoid. When the really hard times hit, though, they are far easier to weather when our bravery muscles are strong. I'm not suggesting that the challenges we face won't sometimes feel cruel, unfair, and disheartening. But I am saying that we can acknowledge these feelings and (here's the brave part) persevere anyway.

Most of all, bravery sets us free. It gives us the power to claim our voice, and to leave behind what makes us unhappy and go for what sparks in our souls. It allows us to see that our gloriously messy, flawed, real selves are in fact the true definition of perfection.

Part Three

Kiss the Perfect Girl Goodbye: The Path to Being Brave

Very early one morning, I was walking through JFK airport in New York, on my way to a speaking engagement in Atlanta. Because I'd gotten up so early to get to the airport—and because I had to go right to the event when we landed—I put my big curlers in my hair and left them there, planning to take them out right when we touched down. As I was going through security, I saw people staring at me and my head full of giant curlers, and I had to laugh. I must have looked a little ridiculous, but you know what? *I didn't care.* I had a moment of absolute giddiness realizing that not caring what other people think had gone from being something I deliberately practiced to being an automatic habit.

It's time we made bravery a permanent habit. And we're going to do it the way we train ourselves out of any bad habit into a better one: by first becoming aware of the behavior you need to change (chasing perfection), making a decision to change (opening this book), then consciously and repeatedly replacing the old behaviors and mindsets with better ones. Eventually, the new and better habits become so ingrained in you that they become a natural way of being.

The strategies in these chapters are here to help you do exactly that. They are a collection of tips, ideas, and practices I've gathered both from experts and from finding my own way from perfect to bravery (again and again and again . . .) to help you develop or reinforce your bravery habit. They aren't meant to be a prescription for "how to become brave"; there's no singular formula for that. What it means to be brave is personal for each of us, so I want you to pick, choose, and adapt the strategies that feel most relevant to you and that speak to what you need most. If saying no causes you anxiety, you may want to focus on the tips in Chapter Eight, "Nix the Need to Please." If fear of rejection is your thing, go right to Chapter Seven, "Get Caught Trying."

For those who want to learn how to build a sisterhood of strength by supporting other women in personal and meaningful ways, Chapter Nine is all about how we can band together to play for Team Brave. And for any of you who still aren't convinced that you'll survive a failure or serious mistake, take a look at the rebound plan in Chapter Ten, "Surviving a Big, Fat Failure."

Within each chapter you'll find several daily practices that you can use in any order, as often and whenever you can. Just like with any form of exercise, the more you practice them, the easier they get, and pretty soon you'll find the iron grip of perfection loosening and the bravery buzz taking hold. Don't worry, I won't ask you to walk through an airport with a head full of curlers (unless you want to), but I promise you, there's nothing more thrilling than the rush you'll get once you start practicing small acts of bravery!

6

Build a Bravery Mindset

I wasn't born brave. In fact, I was pretty timid and fearful when I was young—until the last day of eighth grade when a group of bigoted bitches pushed me too far.

The sun was shining brightly that day, and there was a warm breeze. (Isn't it always beautiful out just before something ugly happens?) Yearbooks were being passed around and the excitement of graduation was in the air. I was leaning up against the wall talking to my friend Phu when they surrounded me—the original mean girls—jeering and calling me a "haji." They were laughing hysterically, taunting me and inviting me to a fight. Yes, a real fistfight.

At first I rolled my eyes. As one of the only Indian families in my neighborhood, I was used to being harassed. Many mornings I stood outside the front of my house helping Mom and Dad clean up the remnants of the previous night's TP-ing or egging. Once, someone spray-painted "dot head go home" on the side of our house. As my dad and I picked the shards of eggshell off our lawn, I wondered if this was what he had imagined for us. My parents came to this country as refugees, fleeing a brutal dictator in Uganda. They were given ninety days to leave, or they would be shot on the spot. Somehow, though, in spite of all the violence they had witnessed, Mom and Dad always chose to show love and kindness.

They relished their freedom in America and assimilated. Dad changed his name from Mukund to Mike, and Mom quietly brushed off insults about her sari and bindi that she faced at the local Kmart. They silently endured such indignities, big and small, and constantly urged my sister and me to do the same.

Usually, I listened. Until finally, I'd had enough. I was tired of being obedient and quiet. So, when the girls told me to meet them that afternoon after school for a fight, I looked them straight in the eyes and said yes.

When the final bell rang, Phu grabbed me and tried to drag me toward the bus, "Let's just go, Resh, you don't need to do this." God, I wanted to get on that school bus so badly, but I couldn't. I knew I was going to get beat up. I knew I wasn't David against Goliath and this wasn't going to be a scene out of *Karate Kid*. I literally had no chance of winning that fight. I was just a small Indian girl, whose Hindu parents had taught her nonviolence. But I couldn't let those girls make me run and hide. So I walked back behind the school and there they were, armed with a Wilson tennis racket, a bat, and a plastic bag full of shaving cream.

Before I could even set down my backpack, the pack of mean girls was coming at me. All I heard were the screams and laughter from the crowd of spectators—that is, almost every eighth grader in our school—that had assembled behind them. Knuckles crashed into my eye, and I blacked out almost immediately. When I came to moments later, the kids were gone; just the cans of shaving cream and empty plastic bags were left behind.

I woke up the next morning in pain and terrified. I had

this beautiful black-and-blue lace dress that I planned to wear to my graduation that Sunday, and now I also had a big black eye to go with it. But the physical pain wasn't the worst part. I was embarrassed. To me, that black eye meant that I had failed at assimilating, at being accepted by my peers. I didn't know how I would walk into that ceremony with my head held high. But I did know that if I *didn't* show up, I would always cower. My graduation was a huge turning point for me. By showing up, I made a decision to be my whole self, even if that meant acknowledging that I had failed at fitting in.

So I pinned my hair in an updo and painted my lips pink and decided I was going to *rock* that black eye. My graduation turned out to be my first failure party. And, honestly, it was the best decision I could have made. I felt bolder and stronger and prouder that day than I ever had, knowing it was better to walk around with a black eye than with a heart full of regret.

The black eye eventually faded, and, sadly, for a long time, the memory of how I felt that graduation day faded, too. You'd think that girlhood experience would have fundamentally changed me, but over time, the memory got buried under the weight of everything I was working so hard to accomplish. It wasn't until that pivotal August day many years later when something in me snapped and said *Enough!* that I remembered how freeing facing my fears had felt. That was when something in me shifted for good and I decided to make a lifelong commitment to bravery.

I've learned that when it comes to being brave, your mindset determines everything. If I'd believed on those two fateful days that I simply wasn't capable of courage—that I just wasn't the type of girl who could stand up for herself against a pack of vicious mean girls, or that I wasn't the type of woman who could quit the life path she'd chosen to make her parents happy and go after what she really wanted—then I would have proven those things to be true. But somehow, I believed I could *grow into* the brave, confident person I wanted to be, and eventually, through lots of failures and rebounds, setbacks and small victories, I did.

Obviously, we can't simply will ourselves to be brave. There's no magic potion, no silver bullet. And it's not like we can do one courageous thing and then we're done. It's a process that we're called to, day after day, and it requires consistent practice. We'll always face new setbacks and bigger challenges, and to meet them requires strategies to cultivate the mindset out of which bravery can become a lifelong habit.

Strategy: Keep Your Tank Full

Every woman I know is exhausted. We do, and take on, so much—between working and being a mom, friend, daughter, mentor, keeper of the family's well-being, pet caretaker, travel planner, and master scheduler. Add to that the stress of trying to do all that perfectly and a deep-seated drive to put others' needs above our own and you've got a recipe for serious burnout.

But here's the good news: the era of burnout as a badge of honor is over. It used to be considered badass to juggle fifty things at once, to work twenty-four seven even if we were on vacation or had the flu, to subsist on caffeine and PowerBars. Not anymore. Now that we know the toll of these depleting habits, workaholism is out and wellness is in. After all, Arianna Huffington, arguably one of the biggest media moguls of our time, wrote a blockbuster bestseller about the power of sleep. That's right: the fifty-second-most-powerful woman in the world according to *Forbes* is on a mission to prove that one of the ultimate secrets to success is getting enough shut-eye. Good enough for me.

It's not just that fatigue costs us and the economy billions of dollars in lost productivity ($411 billion a year, to be exact), or that stress has been linked to serious ailments from obesity to heart conditions, or that we look and feel like crap when we're running on fumes. As Arianna pointed out when I told her I was writing about women and bravery, we can't be brave if we're burned out.

She's right, of course. There's no way you will have the stamina to take risks if you feel like you're out of gas. It's damn near impossible to muster the courage to say no or to try something scary and new when your energy is depleted and your brain is fried. I don't know about you, but when I'm wiped out, the last thing I want to think about is putting myself out there in any way. All I want to do is put on leggings and a sweatshirt, throw my hair up in a bun, swap out my contacts for my dorky glasses, collapse on the couch and escape into the oblivion of Netflix. Exhaustion and being overwhelmed are pretty much instantaneous bravery killers.

It demands emotional and even physical energy, stamina, and endurance to leave our comfort zone, which is why the first and most essential key to cultivating a bravery mindset is to put your wellness first.

Here are the basics:

- **Prioritize your health**. Lianna walked around with a painful sinus infection for four days because she didn't have time to go to the doctor. Yet when her dog got sick and started suddenly vomiting, she immediately dropped everything to run him over to the vet. Sound familiar? It's crazy how many of us shove our basic self-care aside—

and it's no wonder so many of us end up suffering from autoimmune diseases, back pain, depression, or worse. It's brave to say: *no more*. No more showing up for work or to meet a friend when you have the cold from hell just because you didn't want to let anyone down. No more sacrificing your workout plans or a doctor's appointment to accommodate someone else's schedule. You wouldn't ignore a troubling mole on your kid's shoulder, or let your best friend get away with postponing her mammogram because she's too busy, so take an equally powerful stance for your own well-being. Consider prioritizing your health as your first official act of radical bravery.

- **Take that "me time."** A 2012 national study done by the Family and Work Institute proved what we all intellectually know to be true: the women who make it a regular habit to set aside time for themselves are much more satisfied with their lives than those who put it off. But just because we know that relaxing and replenishing is good for us doesn't mean we actually do it. Saying yes to taking care of yourself usually means saying no to someone else in some form or another, and for those of us who are wired to think that prioritizing our needs is selfish, that's really, *really* hard. But that's also what makes it brave.

- **Get some sleep—seriously.** I'm going to go out on a limb and guess that you try to squeeze every last thing you can into your day, from waking up at dawn to work out and make your kids pancakes (even though cereal would be perfectly fine) to staying up late answering emails and cleaning every last dirty dish. Perfectionism compels us to burn the candle at both ends, but don't fool yourself into thinking that you can "get by" on only a few hours of sleep. Studies have shown that seven to nine hours a night is what you need to operate at your best. Being well rested won't automatically make you braver, but I can promise you that *not* being well rested will seriously get in your way.

- **Learn to meditate.** Scientific studies prove that meditation shrinks the amygdala, which is the part of the brain that is driving the bus when we feel threatened or scared. For a small time investment of ten to twenty minutes a day, you can literally rewire your brain to respond to everyday life situations from a place of calm rather than fear.

- **Schedule in gym time.** You knew this was coming. Sorry, but the stats are all true: Exercise has been proven to ward off everything from excess weight to stress to anxiety to disease—all of which influence whether we're feeling empowered or depleted. Besides, nothing makes you feel fiercer than looking in the mirror and seeing a strong, sexy warrior babe reflected back at you. (Just to be clear: we're talking about exercising to feel healthy, inspired, and accomplished . . . *not* to sculpt a perfect body! Keep it real; you know the difference.) As every fitness guru will tell you, the secret to making a fitness routine stick is to schedule it in advance, just like you would anything important.

Strategy: Claim the Power of "Yet"

I'm not brave.
I'm not the kind of person who takes risks.

I'm just not good at saying no.

Declarations like these are the very definition of what it means to be trapped in the fixed mindset I talked about earlier in the book. They leave no room for growth or progress; just a dead end. But look what happens when you add one small word to the end of those statements:

I'm not brave . . . yet.

I'm not the kind of person who takes risks . . . yet.

I'm just not good at saying no . . . yet.

Suddenly, you've gone from stuck to free. You're growing toward something, on your way from where you are to where you might go. Psychologist and motivational pioneer Carol Dweck referred to this as embracing the "power of yet" as opposed to "the tyranny of now."

This small mental shift can have a powerful impact, especially when it comes to reframing mistakes. You didn't "not succeed"—you just haven't succeeded *yet*. When you look at it that way, mistakes don't have to become glaring signs of permanent limitations or failures—they're just temporary setbacks. Less-than-perfect attempts don't have to put a hard stop to the story; instead, you can turn an "I blew it" into an "Okay, tried that, now I'll try something else."

Veronica Roth, author of the blockbuster *Divergent* series, told me that when she was growing up, there wasn't a single area of her life that wasn't touched by her desire to be perfect. Back then, if she wrote a draft that didn't come out so great, she would pronounce the whole thing "garbage." Now, she's trained herself to say, "This draft has potential and just needs to be fixed." In other words, "This draft isn't excellent . . . yet."

None of us is a finished product; we're all works in progress. Next time you catch yourself making a blanket declaration about your limitations, remind yourself of that by adding a "yet" onto the end and you'll immediately feel the difference.

Strategy: Do the "Drama vs. Wisdom" Test

Being thoughtful is smart. It's wise to survey the landscape and weigh the pros and cons before taking any action that involves risk. It's when we overthink, overprepare, and over-analyze that we veer out of cautious territory and into Stucks-ville.

The border between those two zones is marked by fear. The key to crossing it is learning to recognize when you're being wisely cautious and when you're talking yourself out of something just because you're afraid. When you pass on a challenge or an opportunity, ask yourself, *Does this really not make sense to do, or am I not doing it because I'm scared and out of my comfort zone?*

Or, as my brilliant executive coach, Rha Goddess, puts it, "Is that your drama or your wisdom talking?"

You'll know it's your wisdom when you feel at peace with your decision. The voice of wisdom is calm, with a sense of authority. Drama, on the other hand, tends to be a little whinier, more nervous, and more defensive (imagine a guilty Chihuahua and you'll get the picture). If you hear yourself making excuses, find yourself compelled to explain your choice to anyone who will listen, or just feel vaguely disappointed or unhappy, it's a sign that your drama is calling the shots.

I often think about this in weighing whether I want to run for public office again. Up until I started working on this book, I was absolutely sure the reason I wasn't going to run was because I felt like I was making a bigger impact doing what I'm currently doing with Girls Who Code. But after putting the question about drama versus wisdom to hundreds of women, I have to turn the lens on myself and ask, *Is it actually that I'm afraid to fail again?* (The jury is still out on this one.)

The next time you're about to take a pass on something, hit pause and ask yourself if it's your drama or your wisdom that's talking. It's a great way to practice calling bullshit on your automatic excuses and to get real with yourself instead.

Strategy: look for Your ledge

What's the one thing you're most afraid of doing? The thing that if you could do it, you know it would make a major difference for you in your life?

Rha Goddess calls that one thing your "ledge." She says all of us are being called to some ledge, whether we've wanted to consciously acknowledge it or not. I call that ledge "my scary thing." Whatever you call it, she's right that we all have at least one challenge, one change, one move, one dream quietly calling out to us that we're afraid to step up to. I've asked dozens of women the question of what's the one scary thing they could do that would shift things for them in a profound way, and the answers always came quickly. Jillian's one thing is telling her husband about her mountain of hidden debt. For Dawn, it's finding a job that pays more. For Lissette, the ledge is losing the seventy-five excess pounds that are impairing her happiness and mobility. Other women talked about ending toxic relationships, telling grown children they need to move out, taking care of legal issues, or changing their career or other life path. We may not be doing that one big thing (yet!), but deep down, we know what it is, and identifying it is the first step in seeing where we're stuck and what we can work toward tackling.

Where's your ledge that you're being invited to step out onto? If you're not sure, start looking where your comfort zone is; as Rha says, anyplace you're comfortable is a place to be a little bit suspicious. I'm not saying you have to go there just yet—or even at all—but training yourself to at least *look* for it channels your mindset in the right direction.

Strategy: Ask Yourself, What Scares Me More?

A highlight of the 2016 Women's March on Washington for me was the protesters' signs. There were so many smart, defiant, fierce, and funny ones (a personal favorite: "Hands too small, can't build a wall," but that's another conversation). Clever jabs aside, one in particular stood out for me, made by a quiet woman from New Hampshire named Mara. Mara is an introvert who hates big crowds, yet she showed up to bravely stand among the throngs of people filling the streets of D.C. that day. Her sign read, "Crowds scare me. Trump scares me more."

I love this so much more than just a political statement. It's a strategy we can use to put fears into perspective by shifting our focus from what scares us about taking action to what scares us about *not* doing something.

My friend Adam Grant, an organizational psychologist and *New York Times* bestselling author, says that the most brilliant, innovative people are very often procrastinators or afraid of taking risks. So what moves someone to go from just incubating a great idea to putting it out into the world? He says it's the moment when the fear of failure is overtaken by the fear of failing to try. It's when they realize that while they might fail, that's better than failing to matter. Just imagine what you might achieve once you make the shift from worrying about whether you'll make a fool of yourself to instead asking if you'll one day regret never taking the chance.

"A lot of it is doing mental time travel," Adam says. "Being able to mentally fast-forward ten years ahead is one of the most uniquely useful human skills. Maybe right now being told no or failing feels really uncomfortable, but even more uncomfortable might be someone staring back at you ten years from now who was unwilling to pursue that ambition. Mental time travel helps you detach from the immediate consequences of taking that risk and think about it with some perspective: *What will I weight more heavily, the sting of failing, or the pang of what might have been?*

For me the shift happened at age thirty-three. I'd always thought there was plenty of time to run for office, but I woke up one day and realized, *Oh shit . . . I'm not that young anymore.* The thought of running for office scared me, but the idea of running out of time to do so scared me more. Fear of regret can be a powerful motivator.

So can envy. I have a friend who is an amazing writer. She took a job as a journalism professor, but she hates it; all she wants to do is be an author. Anytime someone writes a book that she feels like she could have written, it's like a stab in the heart. While the torture she felt every weekend reading the Sunday *New York Times Book Review* certainly wasn't fun, it did provoke her to finally start working on her own book.

Author Veronica Roth, who suffered from lifelong anxiety and paralyzing self-doubt, eventually had to ask herself which was scarier: putting herself out there, or stifling her voice. "The scary thing about writing is opening yourself up to criticism and being vulnerable with strangers, but it was more important to me to grow as a writer than to avoid criticism," she told me.

I met a woman named Lauren who worried her daughters would grow up to avoid challenges just because they were afraid. So even though the idea of going white water rafting with them on a family trip scared the wits out of her, she went for it. The idea of modeling fear for her girls scared her more than putting on a wetsuit and getting into that boat.

When you smack up against a wall of fear, instead of focusing on what scares you, try taking a step back and asking yourself, *What might the cost be if I* don't *do this . . . and which option scares me more?*

Strategy: Take Your Own Advice

Here's another easy but highly useful tip from Adam Grant:

When you're faced with a "scary" challenge or opportunity and debating what to do, ask yourself what advice you would give someone else in that situation. "On average, we make better decisions for others than we do for ourselves," he explains. "All we need for ourselves is one or two reasons not to do it and we can give up. But if we're giving someone else advice, we can take a big step back and discuss the fundamental reasons why they should or shouldn't do it."

For instance, imagine you're asked to give a presentation at work that pushes you outside your normal comfort zone. Maybe the audience is much bigger than you're used to, or public speaking in front of clients makes you break out in a cold sweat. Left to your own rationalization, you might conclude it's just not worth it and say no.

Now imagine a good friend was the one who was asked to give the presentation and asked what you thought she should do. Chances are you wouldn't say, "Oh jeez, no way . . . forget that." You might point out to her what a great opportunity it is for her to try something new, to overcome her fear, or to get more visibility at work. You'd talk through the pros and cons, maybe even come up with some coping strategies to help her feel more confident.

Amazing how easy it is to encourage the people we love to be brave, isn't it? Even more amazing is what happens when we do the same for ourselves.

Strategy: Set Daily Bravery Challenges

One day, a Girl Scout from Washington, D.C., named Alice Paul Tapper noticed the boys in her fourth-grade class raised their hands much more often than the girls. It bothered her to see the girls staying quiet and she guessed it was because they were afraid their answers would be wrong and they would feel embarrassed, or that they worried they wouldn't be able to get the teacher's attention. Together with her troop, she created a "Raise Your Hand" patch to encourage girls to use their voices. Girls earn the patch by pledging to raise their hands in class and encouraging other girls to do the same. Since then the "Raise Your Hand" patch has caught on with Girl Scout troops all around the country.

If Alice and hundreds of other ten-year-old girls can practice bravery on a daily basis, so can we. I can't promise you a patch for your efforts, but I can promise that with every bravery challenge you take on, that muscle will grow stronger.

As Dr. Meredith Grossman explains, one of the best ways to change what we think and believe is by changing what we do—kind of like changing from the outside in. It's hard to believe something to be true without having the actual experience of it; seeing it in action gives you the proof. You can work hard to convince yourself that you won't forever lose the respect of your colleagues if you say something dumb in a meeting, but until you actually utter something less than brilliant and see that nothing terrible happens, you won't entirely believe it to be true.

There's no set path to "becoming brave" other than taking actions over and over again that reinforce bravery rather than fear. That's why I'm challenging you to choose one strategy each day from the chapters that follow and do it. I've said it before but it bears repeating; bravery is a muscle, the more you work it, the stronger it becomes. By practicing bravery on a daily basis when you're on stable ground, you set yourself up to survive the bigger, unexpected challenges that life will undoubtedly throw your way.

7

Get Caught Trying

Sometimes, the best way to become fearless is to walk straight into the fire of fear. I got my first taste of this on my final day of eighth grade, when I faced down that gang of vicious mean girls who wanted to kick my ass just for being brown, and again when I ignored the political elite who were telling me it wasn't my turn and I should get to the back of the line. I walked into that fire when I tried yet again to get pregnant after three miscarriages, when I launched Girls Who Code even though I knew nothing about coding, and in hundreds of little ways every day since. Practicing bravery in the small ways in my day-to-day life has allowed me to step up and face my larger fears when it counted.

Braving my fear enables me to go after what I want and do what I think is right, even when everything isn't perfectly aligned or guaranteed to work. As I said earlier, in the words of my mentor Hillary Clinton, I'd rather be caught trying than not at all. The strategies in this chapter will help you learn to get comfortable with your own imperfection—and yes, even failure—so you can stop being afraid of it. You've likely heard some version of the adage that bravery is not the absence of fear, but acting in the face of it. Because when you face your fear, you take away its power. That becomes your secret weapon that lets you escape the tyranny of perfection and go after what you really want.

Strategy: Ask for Feedback

For perfection-seeking girls and women, critical feedback is a bitch. If someone gives us anything less than a glowing review, we wither inside and immediately spiral into "I suck." We take it as a permanent indictment of our character. It's sickening, demoralizing, and altogether brutal.

The antidote to this is not to avoid criticism, but to actually invite it. Yes, you read that right: I want you to actively ask for cold, hard, unadulterated feedback. And *not* when you know you've aced something, but when you know you've got plenty of room for improvement. It's kind of like radical exposure therapy to desensitize yourself. It might feel like a swift kick in the gut for an instant, but the more you do it, I promise, you're going to discover really fast that critical feedback doesn't hurt nearly as much as you think it will. Eventually it becomes kind of like a positive addiction: I now actually love getting it because it points me to my next challenge.

Recently I spoke at a rally right after the woman to whom I lost my public advocate race, who happens to be an amazing speaker and knows how to fire up a crowd. It was pouring out, my son had been pulling on my coat to get my attention all day, and I was especially run-down from traveling; to be honest, I'd been doing so much public speaking that I hadn't really given much thought to what I was going to say. I figured, *It'll be fine. I've got this.* After I spoke, I got into the car with my husband and asked him how I did. He looked at me and said, "You kind of sucked."

Um, what?

"You were a two, maybe a three, out of ten," he said (as you can tell, we don't pull any punches in our relationship).

The tough love admittedly didn't feel great in that second—especially since it was an already serious sore spot to face the woman I'd lost my election to. Still, I was really grateful for his honesty. What good would it do me for him to sugarcoat and tell me I was great when I wasn't? For a few weeks after that, I thought long and hard about how I'd gotten into my comfort zone with public speaking and how I could get better in rally formats. I've now gotten excited about recognizing that even if I'm at the height of my game, I can (and should) still find ways to improve.

The key to this strategy is to not just endure feedback, but to actively seek it out all the time, everywhere, from everyone—*especially* when you don't want to hear it. I gave a speech recently in front of four thousand people and got a standing ovation. I was feeling really good about it and didn't really want anything to spoil that, but I still asked my staff to critique me. Why? Because even the best speeches can always be better. I even do this in my personal life; after my husband and I have an argument and the dust settles, I ask him how I could have communicated better.

Angela Duckworth, author of the bestselling book *Grit*, identified the courage to accept feedback as one of the four critical factors for building grit. Those who have grit are constantly looking to improve, so they ask, "How did I do?" Angela points to great athletes as examples. Think about someone like Michael Jordan or Michael Phelps; how did they get that good? First, they focused narrowly on the one thing they wanted to improve on. Then they practiced . . . and practiced . . . with 100 percent focus. But the other key component is that they solicited feedback. They had the courage to face the fact that they weren't perfect—to ask how and where they weren't great—so they could refine and get better. They were living at the cutting edge of their ability and were totally turned on by that.

When you're pushing yourself beyond where you're comfortable and striving for improvement, you're firing on all cylinders. That's when you enter that magical psychological state known as "flow." One secret to getting to that blissful state is to build up the courage to hear feedback, which points you to the next area of improvement, and the next, and the next. The more you do this, the easier it gets, and the faster you'll go from feeling kicked in the gut by criticism to feeling grateful and empowered by it.

Inviting criticism enables you to bear witness to your own imperfections and build a tolerance for them. First tolerance, then acceptance, and then, believe it or not, joy.

Strategy: Surround Yourself with Rejection

Boys and men aren't tyrannized by failure. Because they've been trained from a young age to shake it off and just keep going (a fall off the monkey bars, a science experiment that bombs, a date invitation that gets turned down . . .), mistakes and rejection tend to roll off them in a way that most women can only envy. Our perfect-girl training has kept us safely isolated from the sting of rejection and failure, but as you know, it also weakened our resilience in our adult life. One way we build back our resilience and take the sting out of rejection and failure is by normalizing it.

When Shaan was a baby, our pediatrician told us to skip the excessive use of hand sanitizer and expose him to as many germs as possible to build up his immunity. Much in the same way, we can all immunize ourselves against rejection by exposing ourselves to it. In other words, don't hide from rejection—own it!

Right now on my fridge I still have the original rejection letter from Yale Law School taped up right next to the rejection letter from my community board. Throwing them away gave them too much power over me. Staring them down, however, put me back into the driver's seat. They remind me every day to be brave and keep going.

The more I exposed myself to rejection, the less it terrorized me. I won't lie: there's always been a little undercurrent of a living-well-is-the-best-revenge fantasy there; I dreamed one day of showing these people what I could accomplish, which gave my motivation a little extra edge.

Display your rejections proudly; they're a mark of your bravery. Talk about your rejections, mistakes, and flubs, and invite your friends and colleagues to do the same. Read as many stories as you can about famous and accomplished people who lived through failures, like Stephenie Meyer, whose manuscript for *Twilight* was rejected by twenty publishers before it found a home, or Steve Jobs, who was long ago fired from Apple. Their setbacks didn't destroy them, and neither will yours. In fact, they'll set you free.

Strategy: Get Your Fear Signals Straight

The funny thing about feeling fear is that 99 percent of the time, it's a false alarm. Our nervous system was designed to keep us safe from predators, so anytime we feel afraid, our primitive brain believes we're about to be attacked and sends the signal to run like hell.

The problem, of course, is that your nervous system doesn't know the difference between perceived danger and real danger. Your heart may be hammering and your palms might get sweaty—clear signals from your body that you're in jeopardy—but realistically, standing up to your boss literally will not kill you. The doomsday we fear almost never happens. Your friend isn't likely to disown you forever if you forgot to call when her mom came home from the hospital. You probably won't lose your job if you show up late for a meeting. There's a slim chance your kid's future will be irrevocably destroyed if you accidentally send a snarky email about your kid's teacher to her, instead of sending it to your husband (yes, I did that, and no, Shaan didn't get blackballed).

When we're driven to be perfect, any small flaw or mistake will trigger the alarm and send us running. What we want to do is train ourselves to recognize that, most of the time, we should ignore the alarm because it's not a signal of genuine danger. It's not a tiger that's chasing you—it's your modern-day anxiety.

I love this advice Dr. Meredith Grossman gives her patients: Do the opposite of what your anxiety is telling you to do. Your anxiety will *always* scream at you to run, hide, bail. So don't! If it's telling you to skip that networking event because you'll feel too awkward, go. If it's urging you to spend hours scrubbing down your apartment before your mother-in-law comes over, do a light cleanup and leave it at that. If it's telling you to avoid making a public gaffe at all costs, type gibberish on your Facebook page and post it. It's so liberating to see that, honestly, no one cares. And if they do, really, does it even matter?

Look for whatever makes you feel uncomfortable and go there. Show up ten minutes late without apologizing profusely. Send an inconsequential email with a grammatical mistake in it. Wear a shirt with a stain on it. Leave the house not looking your best. Wear a skirt without shaving your legs that morning. Tell a friend that you're feeling insecure. Practicing imperfection doesn't have to be superhard or grandiose. You don't have to tell your boss to fuck off or become a hot mess in public. Do this in small, low-stakes ways so you can see that you can tolerate the stress. All the microactions we take to prove that our anxiety isn't a reliable narrator add up. This paves the way for bigger and more tolerance of imperfection and, in turn, opens the door for bravery.

Strategy: Start Before You're Ready

Here's what generally runs through our minds when we have a big idea:

> *Oh, wow . . . that could be great.*
> *I should do this.*
> *I'm definitely going to do this!*
> *Wait, but how about . . . ?*
> *I don't know how to. . . .*
> *I can't do . . .*
> *This is probably a dumb idea.*

Almost as soon as a brilliant idea arises, that annoying voice in your head starts yapping about all the reasons you shouldn't do it, what could go wrong, how you can fail, how arrogant you'll seem for trying, and how stupid you will look when you fall on your face. By the time you're done listening, you've talked yourself right out of trying.

The trick to shutting up that annoying voice is to *just start.*

It doesn't matter if you don't know absolutely everything you need to know right now to do a job—whether it's running a company or becoming a mom. Most people don't.

Honestly, I'm not kidding. They pick it up as they go along. Don't know how to change a diaper? You'll learn. Not sure how you'll manage thirty employees? You'll figure it out. You always do, don't you?

By all measures, I never should have started Girls Who Code. Remember, I had no idea how to code, I had never worked in the technology industry, and I had never started a nonprofit. But I couldn't get the image of all those missing female faces in the tech classes I'd visited on the campaign trail out of my head. So I made a few phone calls to solicit some advice from a few people I trust. Then a few more, and a few more. I spent a year meeting with anyone and everyone I could to learn about the tech industry and about teaching girls. Today, Girls Who Code is a global organization that has taught more than ninety thousand girls that they have what it takes to pursue a career in technology, but don't kid yourself that its founder knew what she was doing when she first started.

Cecile Richards, the formidable former president of Planned Parenthood, almost didn't apply for the position. She said her self-doubt kept reminding her how she'd never done anything that big before, and she had a long list of all the things she didn't know how to do. But, as she said, "I went ahead and tried it anyway. If you wait until everything lines up, it's over."

Next time you have that idea or project, instead of talking yourself out of it or putting it off for "someday," just start the process in some small way: make a phone call, buy the URL, write the first paragraph, set up a meeting to talk to some people you trust to get their thoughts. You don't have to tackle the whole thing all at once. Up until pretty recently, I used to be really afraid to ride my bike downhill. Every time I got to a big hill, I'd skip it, and then I'd feel bad. Then I checked myself and saw that my old perfection wiring was steering: if I was going to ride a bike, damn it, then I was going to do it perfectly! But really, why did I have to tackle the HUGE hill? Why couldn't I just start with a small slope, master that, and then go from there?

No more waiting until you're "ready." As Cecile Richards said, if you're waiting for the stars to all perfectly align, you'll be waiting forever. You'll never have the exact right résumé, experience, child-care arrangement, or wardrobe. There is no ideal moment to begin any more than there's the perfect version of you.

Just tackle the small hill first to get the energy moving in the right direction and see where it goes. The worst that can happen is that you fall. But so what? If you don't take those first steps, you'll always wonder what you missed out on. Far better to fall down trying than to never have tried at all.

Strategy: Choose Failure

Yes, you read that right. I want you to *choose* failure—or at least the potential for it.

In the start-up world, you're not taken seriously if you haven't had at least one colossal failure. The unofficial motto in Silicon Valley is "Fail early and often." Almost no one gets it right the first, second, or even third time. Failure is baked into the innovation process; it's how they learn what doesn't work so they can home in on what does. This is why the business world worships serial failures like those of billionaire and Tesla founder Elon Musk, who was ousted as CEO of his own company, fired from PayPal while on his honeymoon, and had to cop to multiple critical malfunctions (and explosions) of his SpaceX rockets. Failure shows you've got what it takes to execute, pivot, crash and burn, and rebound.

Most of us are experts at weighing the pros and cons of an opportunity. A woman I know who works freelance spends *days* debating whether she should take on a project (driving most of her friends nuts in the process). When our careful analysis shows that we could fail, we don't select that option; our perfection wiring urges us to look for a guarantee of success or forget it. Recently, I've gotten a lot of phone calls from women who are thinking about running for office and looking for advice. I always tell them to go for it, even if—*especially if*—their chances of winning are slim, because it's the value of the fight that matters.

Before she was a senator, Elizabeth Warren was a Harvard law professor and bankruptcy specialist turned activist. Beginning in 1995, she was involved in a monumental campaign to stop proposed legislation that intended to make it impossible for hardworking middle-class families in financial peril to file for bankruptcy. Despite her tremendous efforts in leading one of the biggest lobbies in history, they lost the decade-long battle when legislation was passed in 2005.

But, as Senator Warren has said, she's not sorry she jumped into that fight. Now leading the charge in the fight to fix the health-care system in our country, she credits that early loss as an invaluable training ground. Through that experience she learned how to effectively battle for what she believes, made powerful allies, and hatched important new ideas—one of which eventually became the Consumer Financial Protection Bureau. That failure helped her hone her voice and strengthen her bravery muscles—both of which I imagine came in pretty handy when she became a United States senator and famously stood up to the president.

So go ahead and do your risk calculus, same as you always do. Only next time, if it comes out seeming too high, do it anyway (as long, of course, as it's not putting you or anyone else in serious jeopardy). I promise, failure won't break you. Deep down, you know that. Here's your chance to prove it to yourself.

Strategy: Do Something You Suck At

I can remember the first time I tried something that didn't come easily to me. It was in sixth-grade gym class, and I attempted a cartwheel. All the other girls seemed to be able to easily launch their slender legs up in the air and execute a beautiful, graceful spin. But I wasn't a skinny kid, and my one clumsy attempt looked more like I was playing leapfrog than doing a cartwheel. When I stood up, I saw my classmates cracking up and heard one of the popular girls sneer, "That was pathetic." My cheeks burning with shame, I decided on the spot that that was my first and last cartwheel.

Even today, at age forty-two, I catch glimpses of that hot shame creeping in if I can't do something gracefully— especially when I'm comparing myself to others who look like they can. Just this morning I went to spin class and noticed I wasn't doing the moves as well as the woman on the bike next to me. Immediately I started judging myself, feeling bad, wanting to give up. But I didn't, mostly because I'm committed to building my bravery muscle every chance I get (and a little bit because I'm committed to keeping my rear end north of my knees). When I'm feeling over my head—whether in a fitness class or speaking in front of some of the most brilliant minds in technology—I don't fold. I don't pull back or hide, even if I want to.

Doing something that you kind of suck at is yet another way to build a tolerance for imperfection and, in turn, revive the joy that perfection may have strangled. A woman I met named Eva told me that for years, she labeled herself a notoriously bad cook. Nearly everything she tried to make came out burned or tasted awful. Frustrated and defeated, she gave it up. That is, until she became a mom and her five-year-old daughter asked if they could make homemade brownies for the school bake sale. The brownies came out kind of mushy and undercooked, but it was well worth it to Eva for the memory she made with her daughter that day giggling and licking the batter off the mixer.

Fumbling your way through something new isn't just about fun; it also changes your brain for the better. We can literally rewire our brains and what we're capable of, which in turn expands what we *believe* we're capable of. A famous study of London cabdrivers showed that learning the layout of twenty-five thousand city streets markedly increased the area of the brain that controlled their spatial memory. But you don't need to take on such a huge learning curve to benefit; research has shown that gray matter increases after practicing a new undertaking only two times.

If you're a lousy cook, make dinner (and I don't mean by dialing for takeout). If you're not the most coordinated person in the world, go to a CrossFit or dance class (see the next section, "Take on a Physical Challenge"). If you have two left thumbs, take a stab at painting or knitting. If you're still carrying around the "I'm bad at math" block, learn to code (go to www.khanacademy.com). Trust me, nothing will teach you to tolerate mistakes faster than coding!

It's probably time I give that whole cartwheel thing a try again.

Strategy: Take on a Physical Challenge

I was confused. Sitting with the seventh group of women I'd gathered together to talk about perfection and bravery, I found none of the things these women were saying jibed with all the other input I'd heard. When I brought up the topic of rejection, they said they were able to shrug it off by not taking it personally. Failure? Again, not a big deal for them; win some, lose some. Fear of taking risks? Not really, because the worst that can happen is you screw up and just try again.

Then it hit me. This particular group of women all worked in the fitness industry in one capacity or another, from trainer to fitness model to CEO of a national sports club chain and every single one of them had grown up as athletes. I asked about the impact of that and without hesitating, they all said playing a sport as a kid gave them a resilience they draw upon in their everyday adult life.

It turns out that empowering your body empowers your bravery. Sports have been shown to be an invaluable way for girls to build their self-esteem—and sidestep the perfect-girl wiring. On the field or court, there's no room for being nice, polite, sweet, accommodating, neat, and clean. That's where they get to be assertive, competitive, loud; where they get dirty, don't have to hold back or apologize for their talent, and communicate directly and honestly in the interest of building a united team. It turns out that even mastering a physical activity is a *huge* bravery boost. This past summer, my fifteen-year-old niece Maya came to visit us and wanted us to take a surfing lesson together. I hate cold water (anything less than 85 degrees is cold to me), and did I mention I can't swim? But because I hadn't done anything outside my comfort zone in a long time, I said sure, let's do it. I needed to shake things up.

I woke up that morning still pretty excited about doing something new and scary. When we got to the beach, I put on the wetsuit and felt kind of fierce. I loved the superchill energy of the surfer dudes, since I'm normally pretty uptight. We had a brief lesson on the beach and everything was going fine until I had to get in the water. Suddenly I got scared out of my mind and started asking John, my instructor, to tell me all the ways a person could die while surfing, which led to him eventually begging him to take me back to the beach. He was having none of it.

So I got myself into the water and paddled out a bit, finally. The next challenge was jumping up to get on my board, which meant falling into the water over and over. I was annoyed, frustrated, and drenched with saltwater up my nose and stinging my eyes . . . but I kept going. The waves kept crashing on me but I held on, and John kept telling me I was doing, "Awesome!" Trust me, I didn't feel awesome. I *really* wanted to give up.

At one point, I looked to my left at my niece, who is an athlete, so of course she was a total natural at riding the waves. Then I looked to my right and saw—I kid you not—an eight-year-old doing a handstand on his board. I felt like an idiot shaking and swearing like a sailor, clutching my board for dear life. *Come on, Reshma*, I thought. *This is ridiculous. You've tackled harder things than this!* I'd come this far and wasn't going to leave that ocean until I'd gotten up on that board one way or another.

When the next wave came, I hopped up on my two feet and stayed up for about ten seconds before I fell off. It was *thrilling*! I tried five more times, never staying up for more than ten seconds, but I didn't care.

Would I do it again? For sure. I loved the challenge and

the fact that it didn't come easy for me. In fact, I *want* to go back and learn how to get past the fear barriers in my mind. It was an amazing experience, not because I managed to get up on that board (because I didn't, really), but because I didn't give up. I can't remember a day where I felt so free and joyful.

You don't have to try surfing to get this same boost—any physical act of bravery will get you there, as long as it's something that's both challenging and outside your comfort zone. Sign up for a 5K run, take a bike trip, hike a big mountain, chop wood, learn to ice-skate, try indoor rock climbing, take a Zumba class . . . whatever scares you most, that's your ticket. Even if you spent your time as a kid reading instead of running, lack any semblance of hand-eye coordination (guilty on both counts), it's not too late.

Trust me, if I can get myself on a surfboard, anything is possible.

Strategy: Use Your Hands

Anytime Shaan gets a new toy that has to be put together, my first instinct is to tell my husband to do it. Even if I open the box and start the process, almost immediately I get frustrated by how long it takes to figure it out. Hello, perfect-girl training . . . if I can't get it right immediately, I'm outta there.

Same goes for Dimitra. She works in the tech industry, but if her laptop goes down, she immediately turns to her boyfriend for tech support instead of taking the steps to fix it herself. Kate, a wholly capable and competent single mom, told me she has a helpless meltdown anytime an appliance breaks in her apartment. "It's like I turn into a 1950s housewife," she said.

These kinds of tasks have become the territory of men

partially because of old, outdated attitudes about what women can and should do, and partially because as women, we've never been taught to sit with the frustration and challenge that the majority of mechanical tasks require. After all, our society encourages boys to go for it and keep trying even if it's complicated but lets girls off the hook, so we've never really been put into situations where we're told to figure it out. This is the same phenomenon we see in our coding classes; when society is telling girls they aren't good at something, there's no motivation for them to stick with it and work through the problem. Later it colors everything from putting together an IKEA dresser to driving a stick-shift car. So ingrained is our aversion to frustration that not only do we believe we *can't* do these things—we don't want to try!

Don't be a damsel in distress. Building or fixing something with your own two hands gives you power. Computer or phone freezes? Instead of immediately asking someone else to figure it out for you, call tech support and (calmly, with patience) go through the steps to fix the problem. Need to install your toddler's new car seat but are confounded by the instructions? Find a YouTube tutorial and set up that sucker yourself (tip: you can find an instructional video on there for pretty much any task). Empower yourself with the basics to prevent yourself from slipping into old, helpless behaviors: make sure you've got the number for roadside assistance in your phone in case your car breaks down (no, your husband's or dad's phone number doesn't count); take a walk around your house and check the batteries on the smoke detectors; gather up the instruction manuals for appliances and put them all in one place so you can find them when something goes on the fritz.

Learn how to check the air pressure in your tires (*before*

you get a flat); check out a makerspace or sign up for a wood-working class; learn to operate a power drill and put up a shelf in your home; set up that coffee maker that's been sitting in the box since you bought it.

If you get frustrated in the process, remind yourself that you're not aiming to get the gold star here. It's the doing that counts.

8

Nix the Need to Please

l ast year, I was invited to speak at a big tech industry conference. This was shortly after a now-infamous (and hideously inaccurate) memo from a Google employee about why women are biologically unsuited to work in technology was leaked, and just around the time that the first wave of accusations that sparked the #MeToo movement were emerging, so the feminist in me was extra charged up. I guess the guys who ran the conference expected me to give a nice, cheerful talk about girls and coding, but I felt we were in too important a moment to ignore what was happening around us. So instead, I got up onstage and talked about how it wasn't enough for us to teach girls to code, that to level the playing field, Silicon Valley needed to fundamentally change its sexist culture and approach.

When I finished speaking, I didn't exactly hear crickets, but there definitely was no thunderous applause, either; and then my Q&A that was supposed to follow was mysteriously canceled. Behind the scenes it was made clear that the organizers of the event were not happy with me. They thought my talk was inappropriate and that I came across as angry (well, duh). Let's just say there's a more-than-good chance I won't be invited back next year.

In the days after, I was upset. It really irked me how I'd been pressured to fall into line, and I resented the passive-aggressive blackballing that I sensed would be my punishment for daring to be an angry woman. Even more enraging was the thought that they would never slap down a dude for going rogue or being outspoken (in fact, they would probably have applauded it). But mostly, if I'm being honest, I was upset because they didn't like me.

I talked to my executive coach about what had happened, and she said something that really struck home. "The work here isn't to figure out why they didn't like you, or who's right and who's wrong," Rha told me. "It's to practice being okay with the idea that there are some people who will get you and some people who won't . . . *and that's fine*."

Whoaaa.

It had literally never occurred to me that it's perfectly okay if I'm not liked or understood by some; those just aren't my people. There are plenty of others who do get me, and who are aligned with who I am and what I'm here to do.

The more comfortable you get with doing, saying, and being in your truth, the less you'll get caught up in what others think of you. The strategies in this chapter are powerful tools to help you nix the need to please. The irony is that once you free yourself from the need to always be liked, you clear a path for "your people"—the ones who get you—to like you that much more, for all the right reasons.

Strategy: Trust Yourself

Our perfect-girl training has taught us that being accommodating means we agree to go along with what someone else suggests we do, even if deep down we know it's not what we want. We take advice that we aren't really sure feels right, buy the expensive shoes that our friend says we *have to* get (even though we can't really afford them and kind of know we'll never wear them), say the thing our boss thinks we should say to a client even though it doesn't feel entirely genuine to us—often because it's just so much easier to agree than to hurt someone's feelings by saying no.

Early in her career, actress Bridget Moynahan was auditioning for a big role that a guy in her acting class offered to help her with. Every bit of feedback he gave her felt wrong to her, but he'd had success getting work, so she figured he knew what he was doing. She followed his lead—and didn't get the role. "That was a turning point for me about trusting myself," Bridget says. "For me, that's a key element of bravery. You have to trust yourself, whether it's how to play a role or falling in love again even if you've gotten burned. You have to trust that you're going to be okay, that you have something to offer. You need to be brave enough to trust yourself, knowing you'll survive even if it fails."

This strategy is a subtle but crucial one. It requires that you really pay attention to what your gut is telling you, ask yourself whether you're saying yes just to be agreeable, and become aware of when you give away your decision-making power to someone else. Tuning out the urgings of others and listening to our instincts is an important act of bravery.

Strategy: No Fucks Given

Caring about what other people think of us is a habit. It's so deeply ingrained in us to crave the approval of others that we often don't even realize how many of our choices and actions are tied up in that need. One way to break this habit is to be on the lookout for stories of women who do and say what they want, regardless of what others think.

In other words: we need to consciously look for fierce and fabulous examples of *no fucks given*.

I look for stories like these every chance I get—in the news, in stories friends or colleagues tell me, in books I read. I literally collect them and keep both mental and actual files as inspiration. It isn't that hard, really, because if you look around, you'll see plenty of examples everywhere, every day. I will never forget the awe I felt in the 1980s watching Madonna unapologetically break every taboo by writhing around onstage wearing religious ornaments, or the amazement I felt in 2016 witnessing Beyoncé command dancers in Black Panther berets into formation and giving a Black Power salute at the Super Bowl halftime show. Stand-up comic Amy Schumer routinely says whatever she wants, no matter how shocking. Frances McDormand blew off the norm of Hollywood polished glam and accepted the 2018 Golden Globe for Best Actress with zero makeup and tousled hair, then gave a wild and fierce Oscar acceptance speech in support of women in her industry. During a House Financial Services Committee hearing, Congresswoman Maxine Waters refused to let Treasury secretary Steve Mnuchin derail her line of questioning with flattery, pressing for answers and pointedly declaring she was "reclaiming her time." Kiran Gandhi shocked the world when she ran the 2015 London Marathon while "free flowing" on her period to make a statement about the shaming of the processes of women's bodies. Caitlin Jenner blew up the legend of decathlon winner Bruce Jenner to proudly claim her authentic gender identity, right on the cover of *Vanity Fair*. Like I said, no fucks given.

Then, there's the indomitable Dame Helen Mirren. Though

she's famous today for her fierce candor, that wasn't always the case. When a reporter asked her what advice she would give to her younger self, she replied that it would be to not be so "bloody polite" and say "fuck off" more often.

You don't have to agree with these women, or even like them (they don't care if you do, anyway). But you do have to admire them for caring more about what matters to them than what other people think.

Start making it a habit to find examples of women who don't give a fuck what anyone thinks. It's a powerful way to train your brain to focus less on what others think and more on who and what you want to be.

Strategy: Ask "And Then What?"

Our deep longing to be liked is utterly human, a relic of pre-historic days when being accepted (and therefore protected) by your clan literally meant the difference between life and death. Here in the twenty-first century, though, your survival is rarely if ever at stake just because someone thinks you're a bitch. So why, exactly, do we as women so desperately need to be liked?

Each one of us has our own individual reasons why we need others to like us—all of which are driven by what we're afraid will happen if they don't. Think about one specific area in your life where you care most if you're liked (hint: it's usually the space in which you twist yourself into a pretzel to be nice/funny/accommodating, or smile when you really want to scream). Maybe it's at work, or in your mommy and me playgroup, with your in-laws or stepkids, with employees or authority figures, in romantic relationships or friendships.

Got one in mind? Good. Now ask yourself: *What* exactly *am I afraid will happen if this person/these people don't like me?* For instance, "I'm afraid if the moms at my kid's school don't like me, my son won't be invited on playdates," or "If my employees don't think I'm supercool and amazing, they won't work as hard for me."

Now go deeper. Take it to the absolute worst-case scenario by continually asking, "And then what?" For instance:

> *I'm afraid my boyfriend will be annoyed if I tell him I'm pissed off.*
> And then what are you afraid will happen?
> *He'll break up with me.*
> And then what?
> *I'll be alone.*
> And then what?
> *I may never meet anyone else and end up alone forever.*

Ouch. See how fast we take it from zero to sixty, casting ourselves out into the dark void of shame, ruin, and eternal solitude?

Here are some other real-life mental spirals women have shared with me:

> *I'm afraid if the moms at my son's school don't like me, they won't invite him on playdates.*
> And then what?
> *He'll have no friends.*
> And then what?
> *He'll have a sad childhood.*
> And then what?
> *He'll end up on drugs or depressed as a teenager.*

*If I call out my colleagues for making sexist jokes, I'll be
    "that woman."*
And then what?
No one will want to work with me.
And then what?
I'd lose my job.
And then what?
I'll have no money and lose my house.

It's pretty powerful to see for yourself how deep that "be liked or be damned to hell" hardwiring goes—and, more importantly, how preposterous your worst-case scenario really is. Honestly, is he *really* going to dump you if you tell him you're angry? And even if he does (besides him being an ass not worth your time), does that *really* mean you're going to die alone? Is your son *really* going to be ostracized if the other moms don't like you, and even so, is he *really* going to become a heroin addict because he didn't go on playdates with the alpha moms' kids?

We've sold ourselves on the narratives we've created around what it means if we're not liked, but we need to question if those are true. Playing through these scenarios helps you shrink the overblown fear and look at them through the lens of what might actually happen, instead of what you're terrified of.

Look, I'm not saying that there are never consequences. If your boyfriend is an ass, then indeed he might dump you. If your work atmosphere is truly sexist, then it's not impossible you could be asked to leave if you call them out on it. For all these worst-case scenarios, though, ask yourself again, *And then what?*

You'll survive and move on to people who get you, that's what.

Strategy: Just Say No

I really have a problem saying no. I don't want people to think that I'm too big for my britches, or that I'm mean or ungrateful in any way. When I first started Girls Who Code, a high-powered woman in the industry was such a bitch to me, and so I vowed that from that day forward, I would never behave like that toward anyone else.

So now I say yes all the time—at work, to favors, to anyone who asks for a few minutes of my time for advice. I say yes to speaking events halfway across the globe even it means I'll be exhausted and to exploratory meetings with friends of friends that I could delegate to someone on my team. Like you, probably, this is something that drains my time and energy and leaves me depleted. It's also something I'm working hard on changing.

It takes courage to say no—especially when others want or expect you to say yes. Rha Goddess says it's the bravest thing a woman can do, and I'd have to agree. All our perfect-girl tendencies are tied up in saying yes or no to requests: the pressure to be accommodating, to be helpful, to be nice, to be selfless and put others' needs above our own.

I've learned to look at saying no as a value calculation. I ask myself: *What are the things that are the highest value for me? What aligns with my purpose?* This helps me find the line between supporting others but not to my own detriment. Remember back in Chapter Six when we talked about asking "What scares me more?" That's a value question. Only here, the question is, "What am I giving up/not doing by saying yes? What matters more?"

My two highest priorities in my life are my family and making a difference in the world. So I try—and I stress *try*, because this is a work in progress—to make choices that serve those priorities and say no to the things that don't. Turns out it's pretty easy to tell the difference; when I say yes to activities that are aligned with my purpose of being a loving mom and wife or to meetings that move my company's agenda forward, I feel excited, energized, and joyful. But when an entire day goes by and most of that time was spent on what mattered only for someone else, I'm exhausted and grumpy. We've all had the feeling of coming home after a long day feeling like we've been run over by everyone else's agendas, and pissed off that we've ignored our own. At the very least, we can all use days like these to make better choices about what we'll say yes or no to the next day, and how and to whom we'll devote our time and energy.

Recently I got an email from a woman inviting me to an event she had organized. I don't know her personally; she got my name through a professional organization we both belong to. Her email had come in during a moment when I was seriously up to my eyeballs in work and other commitments, and I didn't have a chance to respond. Then I got her follow-up email, in which she informed me, in all caps (i.e., yelling), how disappointed she was that I didn't attend, and she inferred that I broke some unspoken code of conduct of the group we belong to. As I read it, all I could think about was how sick to my stomach with shame and guilt I would have been if I'd gotten that kind of admonishment five years ago. Not that I love being bitched out now, but after working damn hard on becoming brave enough to put my agenda first, I don't take that kind of thing too personally anymore.

Saying no is hard at first; I won't lie. It's one of the biggest challenges we face on our path to becoming brave, but it's also the most gratifying. It's remarkably empowering to claim your right to put you and your life priorities above the mandate of making nice for the sake of everyone else.

Strategy: Make the Ask

If the idea of asking for what you want is painful for you, you're not alone. We perfect girls tend to feel horrified by the idea of seeming pushy, needy, demanding, obnoxious, entitled, or aggressive. Those are not "pleasing" qualities. But you're not here to please everyone else; you're here to build your bravery muscles. So it's time to get in the habit of asking.

Start small by asking for one thing each day that's a little bit outside your comfort zone. If your food arrived cold, ask your waitperson to take it back to the kitchen and have it reheated. Ask a colleague to take a few minutes to read over something you're working on and offer some thoughts. Ask a friend (who reasonably can do so) to drive you to the airport. Invite someone you want to get to know better to have a cup of coffee with you. If you're worried about coming across as pushy, don't. Research has shown that people routinely see themselves as far more assertive than others do. So your version of "pushy" is really probably just normal to everyone else.

Then go bigger. Negotiate for a better price on a car. Request the plum assignment. Ask your significant other to stop doing something that's driving you nuts. Request a meeting with someone you'd like to mentor you. Petition for the flexibility you need at your job.

Here are a few tips I've learned to make asking easier and more effective:

- **Start with "I."** For instance, "I would appreciate if you could take a look at this report" or "I was wondering if you might like to get coffee sometime." This puts you in the driver's seat.

- **Be direct and clear about what you're asking for.**
No beating around the bush or making the person guess
what you're asking.

- **Be respectful.** This is a sign of strength, not weakness.
Saying "please" and "thank you" shows grace and class.

- **If you tend to get nervous, practice** what you want to
say in advance so you're not fumbling for words.

- **Don't automatically offer an out.** I can't tell you how
often employees will ask me for something and then immediately backpedal by saying, "But if it's not possible,
that's okay." Just ask and then be quiet; let the person
answer for themselves.

- **Don't apologize for asking.** No request should start
with "I'm sorry, but would you mind . . . ?"

Strategy: Nevertheless, Persist

Who knew Mitch McConnell, of all people, would hand
women such an empowering rally cry when he disparaged
Senator Elizabeth Warren for pressing her line of questioning
in a hearing after being told to sit down and be quiet? It's not
all in our heads that men try to bulldoze women out of their
voices. As an article in the *New York Times* reported, "Aca-
demic studies and countless anecdotes make it clear that being
interrupted, talked over, shut down or penalized for speaking
out is nearly a universal experience for women when they are
outnumbered by men."

To that I say: The bulldozers have had their day; now it's
our time.

For every time you've ever been silenced or interrupted,
it's time.

For every time you've felt too intimidated or scared of being not liked if you spoke up, it's time.

For every accomplishment you've glossed over out of modesty, it's time.

For every moment you've played nice and swallowed your truth, it's time.

For every time you've stayed quiet when you knew with every fiber of your being you should have spoken up, it's time.

It's time to claim your voice in any and all of these ways:

- **If you have something to say, say it.** If interrupted, *keep talking.* If they tell you to be quiet, *keep talking.* If they call you a "Nasty Woman," say "thank you" and *keep talking.* After being released from spending seven years in a military prison for leaking classified documents, Chelsea Manning faced an onslaught of pressure to shut up and go away. She refused. For her, the fact that everyone was telling her not to speak up was exactly the reason why she believed she should. Amen, sister.

- **Reclaim your time.** I realized recently that I often hurry through my speech when giving a keynote or speaking on a panel because I don't want to take up too much of people's time. None of the men I've ever seen up on a podium or stage do this. They spread out their papers, stand or sit with a more open posture without worrying about taking up too much space, take a long, slow drink of water, and then once they finally start speaking, they take their sweet time. So I'm working on slowing down when I speak. In honor of Congresswoman Maxine Waters, let's all reclaim our voice, our space, *and* our time.

- **Promote yourself.** Studies show that women who are most proactive about making their achievements broadly known get ahead faster, make more money, and are happier overall with their careers. In Silicon Valley, for example, visibility was shown to be a top criterion for promotion to senior levels. Sadly, other studies tell us that women are highly reluctant to talk about their own accomplishments because of that deeply seeded modesty and that voice constantly whispering in our ear, "Don't brag . . . it's not becoming." Here's where we need to take a page from the playbook of men, who have no problem broadcasting their achievements. Close a big deal? Tweet it out. Get a promotion? Send an email to let people know and submit it to your main industry newsfeed so they can publish it. And don't stop there: ask other people to share your good news, too. Anytime someone I admire and respect asks me to shout out the great things that happen to them, I'm happy to do it, and I'm guessing the people in your life will be, too.

- **Spit out the salty lemonade.** Remember the study from Chapter One, where girls choked down salted lemonade because they didn't want to make the researchers feel bad by telling them it was gross? Well, here we are as grown-up women and it's time to spit that lemonade out. In other words, when someone tells you something that you know is wrong, call them out on it. If someone tries to intimidate you into seeing something their way, stand strong. When the cross-examining attorney tried to discredit Taylor Swift during her trial against a radio host who had grabbed her ass during a photo op, she was having none of it. Fielding insulting question after question, she shut him down like a boss. My favorite: When he pointed out, as though it was proof of his client's innocence, that her skirt didn't look as if it was disrupted in any way in the photo, she calmly replied, "That's because my ass is located in the back of my body."

- **Articulate your agency.** Like so many others, when I read the blog post accusing actor Aziz Ansari of sexual harassment for not picking up on his date's "nonverbal cues," I was upset and conflicted. Nearly every woman I know, myself included, has had an experience where someone said or did something that made us feel uncomfortable and we didn't speak up. From the rude and inappropriate to the physically threatening, too many of us, like the woman who wrote the story, have found ourselves in a situation with a guy pressuring us to do something we didn't want to do but didn't overtly say no. Why didn't she—or we—just get up and leave? Why didn't we—or she—speak up? Because we'd never been taught how. No one told us it was okay to have the agency to say *no, get off me, that was inappropriate,* or *fuck off.* So I'm here to tell you it's more than okay. It's your right. The "me too" rage that's been unleashed is the product of decades of pent-up frustration and buried shame from these moments. We're marching with pitchforks to reclaim that power, and now we need to do it by bravely claiming our voice each and every time something like this happens. Time's up, indeed.

9

Play for Team Brave

When Shalene Flanagan blazed past the finish line in 2017 to become the first American woman to win the New York City Marathon in forty years, she did more than just set a record. Her achievement brought to light what the *New York Times* dubbed the "Shalene Flanagan effect," which broke the every-woman-for-herself mold that was pervasive in the professional running world. Instead, she banded female athletes together to push, support, and inspire one another to win. As a result of her efforts, Flanagan and her teammates are now ranked as some of the world's best long-distance runners, winning everything from marathons to Olympic medals.

This is what it means to play for Team Brave. I believe so strongly that the way to change the global landscape for all women is by supporting and pushing one another in personal and meaningful ways. When we encourage each other to be brave and share the results—both the good and the bad—we build a sisterhood of strength that supports us to take on even more courageous acts.

Being brave is a powerful form of activism. When you break ground and become the first to do anything, whether it's winning a marathon or telling someone that the sexist comment he just made wasn't appropriate, it opens the door for other women to do the same. That's how we all get stronger, one brave act at a time.

Strategy: Show the Mess Behind the Scenes

Hanging on the wall in the offices of popular media company theSkimm is a framed copy of a *Vanity Fair* article featuring its two founders, Danielle Weisberg and Carly Zakin. The powerhouse millennial duo are smiling broadly in the photo, looking casually professional, calm, and confident. I was visiting Danielle and Carly to talk about the perfection trap women face, and Danielle immediately pointed to the article on the wall and started to laugh. It turns out that while the women in the picture were projecting an air of effortless success, they were still in hard-core fight-for-your-life start-up mode and had actually had their credit card declined less than an hour earlier.

"I met a female tech entrepreneur recently who said she wanted to hate us, because we make it look easy," Danielle said. "I was stunned by that, because of course it's not true. I feel bad if we've put that image out there because it's equally important to show every Advil-inducing moment along the way. Glamour jobs are never quite what they seem."

There is no such thing as effortless perfection. No one wakes up looking flawless. No couple "never fights," no one's child is a perfect angel, no one landed in the C-suite or at the top of the masthead without breaking a sweat or clawing through some serious setbacks along the way. Instagram filters go a long way toward making us believe that every perfect picture is a snapshot of an equally perfect life, but we know better. Everyone—and I mean *everyone*—is imperfect. Everyone struggles. Everyone screws up. Everyone says stupid things or yells at their kid or forgets to send in their quarterly taxes. Everyone has little secrets they squirrel away shamefully; whether it's that we're in therapy, or that we sometimes stress-eat excessively or that we cry sometimes in the bathroom at work.

We already know the energy and effort it takes to maintain the illusion of perfection—and how empty that struggle ultimately is. The braver step is to let others see that we're human: we struggle; we make mistakes; we fail. What if we could finally let down our "perfect" veneer and allow people to see the messiness behind the scenes?

First, it would relieve us of the heavy armor we've been dragging around with us. That casing weighs a ton. It's a giant relief just to be real.

It would allow us to connect with people authentically, rather than in a hollow and superficial way. If you think about the relationships that make you feel energized, happy, and inspired, they are the ones where there's no bullshit or pretense. No one is *trying* to be anything or look any particular way. No one is looking to impress anyone or be anything other than exactly as silly and human as we all are.

And showing the mess behind the scenes allows everyone else around you to relax and do the same. I know a woman who throws the most amazing political fund-raising parties. Everything always looks impeccable, from the flowers to the food to her hair and makeup. But if you compliment her and marvel at how perfect everything is, she's quick to laugh and tell you that the cat threw up on the rug just before everyone got there or that her gorgeous dress is on loan from Rent the Runway. She's utterly real and maintains a sense of humor about the hard work it takes to make everything look fabulous. In my mind, that humility, that realness—not the impeccable decor or the mouthwatering menu or the expensive china—is what makes her the perfect host.

Don't hide your mistakes in shame—display them with pride! It's brave to reach for something out of your comfort zone, and even braver to let the world see (and commiserate or laugh along with you) when you fall flat on your face. By all means, share your successes, but also share the embarrassing *oops* and *oh shit* moments that got you there. Remember Carly and Danielle's tradition at theSkimm of passing around the "Fail So Hard" hat at their weekly staff meetings for people to put on and share their messiest moment of the week; borrow that tradition and make it your own. My staff and I have started posting #failurefriday moments on social media to get this started . . . come join us.

The point is to just take a deep breath and let people see the real you. You're being brave by letting yourself be vulnerable and, because authenticity inspires authenticity in others, you're paving the way for other women to be, too.

Strategy: Support the Sisterhood

I hate to say this, but bitch culture is never more vicious than when it's woman against woman. Even though it's been proven anecdotally and in research that mentoring one another benefits everyone, we still compete like she-gladiators and craftily tear each other down—usually behind the scenes, through snide comments, gossip, maneuvering, and manipulating. It's death by a thousand cuts, executed through whispers in the ladies' room, passive-aggressive emails, backhanded compliments, icy snubs, and withering comments disguised as "constructive criticism."

I remember so clearly when *The Devil Wears Prada* came out. Pretty much every woman I know had a story to tell about her own Miranda Priestly who tortured her in one way or another. A friend with one of those coveted jobs as an assistant at a talent agency had (on more than one occasion) a cell phone thrown at her by her frustrated female boss. Another who worked in retail stood stunned and speechless as her manager reamed her out for a mistake that the manager herself had made to cover her own ass, in front of an important customer. It's no wonder that the majority of women report that they'd rather work for men than for other women.

There are lots of theories about why we undermine and sabotage each other like this. Some rightly point to the very real obstacles to gender equality that still exist in the workplace. We live in a culture where women need to work twice as hard to earn half the same respect (and less than three-fourths of the same pay), so perhaps we try to hold each other back because every inch of advantage matters. Maybe it's the undercurrent of that double bind of needing to be assertive and bold to get ahead, but then reviled and criticized for being so. Some claim that women are biologically programmed to compete with one another, just as we did back in primitive times when winning the affection of the alpha male—and the protection and resources that came along with that—was paramount for survival.

But underneath all those theories is one unifying truth: we're scared of being outshone, outranked, outdone, or knocked down by another woman, so we strike first. Scared that others will see our imperfections, we make sure to shine a big spotlight on others' flaws. Scared to trust and collaborate with other women, we stick to the every-woman-for-herself style of combat. Feeling vulnerable, we lash out, abuse, and sabotage, doing the very things that we most fear other women will do to us.

What if we looked at this a different way? What if we

viewed supporting other women as a show of strength rather than weakness? What if we worried less about our imperfections and instead focused on enhancing our skills, and helping other women do the same? What if, instead of feeling intimidated by an assertive woman and bitching about her behind her back, we talked about how we admire her instead? What if, instead of worrying there isn't enough room at the top for all of us (and by the way, there is), we went out of our way to help a female colleague or friend get there? What if, instead of feeling "less than" some other woman, we reminded ourselves that we are equally smart/talented/valuable and asked her to collaborate with us instead?

Generosity and bravery are intertwined—especially when it comes to women supporting other women. As many of us know all too well, the drive to be perfect can also drive us to want to be "the best." Giving your time or energy to support other women is brave because it calls you to put aside your quest to be better than everyone else and help make another woman's experience better instead.

In your everyday life, look for opportunities to lift up, mentor, applaud, promote, and support other women. Here are a few ideas to get you started:

- **Brag about each other.** Any time a friend or colleague does something amazing, be their cheerleader and let the world know. If your assistant gets into grad school, post a note on her Facebook wall singing her praises. When a coworker gets promoted, send an email to everyone you work with and invite them for after-work drinks to celebrate. If a woman in your industry wins an award, tweet out a congratulatory note. This kind of support is contagious and will undoubtedly spread, hopefully far and wide until we all get it that we're playing for Team Brave together.

- **Share your random acts of bravery.** The fastest way to inspire other women to be brave is by example. If they can see it in you, they can be it themselves. So share your acts of bravery with your friends, family, and colleagues and let them be *your* cheerleader.

- **Be a bravery mentor.** If you see a woman struggling to speak up or be assertive, reach out and offer to help. If you can tell she's nervous about giving a speech, ask if she'd like you to look over her notes or to be a practice audience. If a friend tells you she would love to take a dance class but is afraid to make a fool of herself, offer to go with her and make fools of yourselves together. Or if she tells you she's been putting off making an important doctor's appointment because she's scared, make her promise to do it *today*, and hold her to it.

- **Give honest feedback.** If a woman asks you what you think, tell her the truth. Don't tell her a white lie to protect her feelings—that compromises both of you and helps no one. You don't need to be harsh to tell the truth; just be direct, calm, fully honest, and respectful.

- **Take her seriously.** If a woman asks you a question, or asks for your advice or input, don't blow her off—you never know how scary it may have been for her to ask in the first place. Whether you agree to her request or not, don't ignore it; none of us is too busy or important to give another woman that level of respect.

- **Form a bravery club.** Just like ten-year-old Alice Paul Tapper, who launched a Girl Scout patch to encourage other girls across the country to raise their hands in class, pull together women you know and launch a bravery initiative. Make a pact to do one brave act every day, and set up a chat group to share your daily acts of bravery.

- **Be a connector.** Know someone who could help out with a project that a colleague is working on? Make the introduction. Have some research that could help make a colleague's work better? Offer it to her. Be generous with your resources and your network by sharing not just what you know, but who you know. The old boys' network encourages men to be abundant with their networks, and we need to be, too.

10

Surviving a Big, Fat Failure

S o you went down in flames. Welcome to the Big Fat Failure Club! It's a club no one ever hopes to be a member of but almost inevitably gets invited to join at some point. We will all experience crushing disappointment at one time or another, whether it's losing an election or a job, bombing an interview or presentation, not getting into the school of our dreams, or seeing our relationship, business, or big plans go up in smoke.

When you're in the midst of despair, it can feel like you'll never recover. But just like that first crushing heartbreak back in middle school that you swore you'd never survive, somehow, you do. Everything you're doing now to strengthen your bravery muscles will go a long way toward getting you through and out the other side.

This step-by-step guide will help you find your way through when things don't go quite as you'd hoped or planned.

Step One: Throw a (Short) Pity Party

The morning after I lost my big race for Congress, I woke up in a hotel room alone, still in the "victory dress" I'd worn the day before, surrounded by the debris of what was supposed to be a celebratory party. My head throbbing and heart heavy as a stone, I somehow managed to get myself up and back to my apartment, where I immediately tossed my crumpled clothes on the floor, put on sweats, and climbed into bed. I pretty much stayed under the covers for the next three days nursing my bruised ego, only crawling out of my hole long enough to consume some Wheat Thins and Diet Coke before getting right back in and resumed mindlessly staring at the television. I felt like complete and utter crap, and probably looked like it, too.

Eventually, I got myself up, turned off the TV, and washed my hair. After a last round of fresh tears and a good strong cup of coffee, I slowly started making the necessary calls to thank my supporters and donors—and you know the rest of the story from there.

Looking back, I absolutely believe that those days I spent wallowing in pity were every bit as essential for my rebound as all the other steps I took next. So I say go ahead and throw yourself a pity party. Allow yourself a finite amount of time to really mourn what you lost (for big painful setbacks I usually go with three days). Put on your comfiest sweats, call your best girlfriends to cry or scream, binge-watch *The Crown*, crack open a bottle of wine, eat Ben & Jerry's right out of the pint—whatever your creature comforts are, go there.

Then, and only when you're good and ready, get up, toss away the empty ice cream containers, and move on to Step Two.

Step Two: Celebrate Your Failure

In the world of scientific research, much like in Silicon Valley, repeated failure is a given. Sometimes, the studies and trials pan out, resulting in millions of lives helped or saved and even more dollars earned; more often than not, they don't.

Yet those failures are still celebrated. Why? Because as Merck's director of neuroscience said, "You celebrate the achievement of getting an answer." Even if that answer isn't the one you'd hoped for.

In 2013, the outlook was promising for Biogen's new drug to treat ALS (amyotrophic lateral sclerosis; also called Lou Gehrig's disease). Early study results were encouraging—a rare ray of hope for sufferers of this debilitating disease—so the company launched a final-stage clinical trial. Patients and doctors around the world hoped and prayed that this would finally be the breakthrough they had been waiting for. When the eagerly anticipated trial failed, the devastated scientists broke down in tears.

Then they went out for drinks.

I wasn't there, of course, but I can just picture these brilliant men and women raising their glasses with heavy hearts, not just to commiserate in their disappointment but also to honor the victories they'd had along the way. I'll give cheers to this team myself, because I know all too well how vitally important this kind of closure can be. Celebrating small accomplishments—even in the face of big failures—is what enables us to press on and hold on to hope that eventually our efforts will result in a breakthrough success.

If you failed, it means you tried. If you tried, it means you took a risk. Celebrate the fact that you put yourself out there and dared to go for it. That's damn brave, woman! Take time to honor that. Celebrate the fact that you got a result, even if it wasn't the result you'd hoped for, because it means you saw something through to its conclusion and can now pivot to your next move.

Step Three: Shake It Off (literally)

In the weeks following the leaked memo by Google employee (now former employee) James Damore that claimed women were biologically unsuited for careers in tech, a tornado of responses hit airwaves and newsfeeds. Like so many women in my industry, I was outraged, so I channeled my disgust into an op-ed for the *New York Times* that took on the memo, point by point. The editors at the paper were superexcited about the piece, as was I, and planned to run it on Sunday, August 13.

The afternoon of Saturday, August 12, our country watched horrified as a white supremacist at a rally in Charlottesville, Virginia, mowed down protesters, killing one woman and injuring dozens more. Needless to say, the op-ed pages quickly (and appropriately) shifted their focus to the deeply troubling race relations in America, and my piece got pulled. Of course I completely understood—I was as sickened by the events as the rest of our country. Still, I was disappointed that something I'd worked really hard on and felt so passionate about would never see the light of day.

I sat on my couch feeling bad for about a half hour (a very brief pity party), then got up and laced up my sneakers to go out for a run to shake it off.

When I say, "shake it off," I mean *literally* shake off the disappointment, shame, or regret that's clinging to you and preventing you from moving forward. Research has shown that physical activity after an emotional blow is key for promoting resilience, so get moving. Go for a run or a long walk, hit the gym, do yoga; even better, do it with friends (strong social connections are another proven resilience booster). If exercise isn't your jam, go do anything that gets you out of your head and back into self-care. Make or bake something. Read an inspiring book. Meditate. Spend an afternoon in the park with your kid. Go to a museum, a movie, a concert.

Will doing these things suddenly make everything peachy again? No, of course not. But it will jolt you out of the funk you're mired in. It'll help refuel your tank and give you the energy and strength to move ahead to Step Four.

Step Four: Review, Reassess, Realign

It's go time. Here's where you make like Beyoncé and turn that proverbial lemon into lemonade.

First, review. The key to this step is to tell or write your story of what happened with as little editorializing as possible. Include just the objective facts, with no blame, or interpretation—as though you were a journalist doing the reporting in the most objective terms. Ask yourself:

- What happened?
- Where, when, how did it happen?
- Who was involved?
- What are the (real, actual) consequences?
- What needs to be changed, repaired, or put back on track?

Second, reassess. This requires what psychologists call "cognitive flexibility," which is a fancy way of saying having the ability to see the situation through a different lens. Psychotherapist Esther Perel refers to it as "reframing your narrative." It's easy to fixate on a single narrative, replaying it over and over in our mind. But when we get stuck on a single, black-and-white version of events—especially one distorted by shame or self-doubt—it limits our ability to see the shades of gray around us. That's when we need to reframe it by taking a step back and asking some broader questions:

- You know what went wrong. But what also went right?
- You didn't achieve what you set out to. What did you learn or gain in its place?
- You've beaten yourself up enough by this point, I'm sure; now it's time to show compassion and let yourself off the hook, same as you would a friend. What worthy efforts and actions did you take that need to be acknowledged? What are you proud of having done? The key to self-forgiveness is focusing on what you did right and remembering that *no one*—not even you—is perfect.
- You got crushed, screwed over, rejected; this is the disempowering blame game. Shift out of blame and into responsibility and ask: What could you have done differently, and what will you do differently next time?
- The walls came crashing down, but what's still standing? What can you salvage?
- You didn't get what you wanted. Is there any upside to it not working out?
- This is the end of one chapter, not the end of the whole story. What could the next chapters be?

Last, realign. Three factors that have been proven to help us bounce back from setbacks are having a sense of purpose, gratitude, and altruism. We realign with our purpose by remembering *why* we took on this challenge in the first place. When I lost my election, I went back to what drove me to run for office, which was a deep desire to serve others and make a difference. Then I redirected my efforts in another direction that allowed me to serve, only in a very different way. In an inspiring TED talk, bestselling author Elizabeth Gilbert shares how she rebounded after her second book bombed. She said, "I will always be safe from the random hurricanes of outcome as long as I remember where I rightfully live." Her love of writing is her "home"—her purpose—her reason for trying. What's yours?

Gratitude is a potent and proven way to shift your mood and energy, because it's not possible to feel bummed out and grateful at the same time. After the painful and public flop of her movie *Beloved*, Oprah Winfrey fell into a depression. But when she eventually pulled herself out, the tether she tied herself to was gratitude. "That's when the gratitude practice became really strong for me," she said, "because it's hard to remain sad if you're focused on what you have instead of what you don't have."

The best way to practice gratitude is to make a daily list. I started doing this every morning about a year ago and I can tell you it has 100 percent made a difference in how I launch into my day. Every morning or evening, write down three things you are most grateful for—and I mean *truly* grateful for. It's easy to just tick off, "my health, my family, my job," and if those are your top three, fantastic. But it's even better to dig a little deeper into specifics. What is it about your family that you are grateful for? (i.e., how they make you laugh, their support, coming home to them every night . . .) What aspect of your job do you appreciate? (the satisfaction of the work, your colleagues, the snacks in the break room . . .) What experience had a positive impact on you? (a book you loved, conversation you had, food you enjoyed, a trip you took . . .) Which elements of your health do you most value? (not being ill or injured, being physically able to do the things you love, feeling energized . . .) What circumstances do you have and hold as personally meaningful? (the unconditional love of your partner, the support of your friends, your comfortable home . . .)

I often put the screwups and setbacks of my day on that list, too, because while I might not be feeling particularly grateful for them at the time, I've learned that every one of them ends up shaping who I am and who I become. I picked up this tip from Ralph Waldo Emerson, who once said, "Cultivate the habit of being grateful for every good thing that comes to you, and to give thanks continuously. And because all things have contributed to your advancement, you should include all things in your gratitude."

Last, altruism is a guaranteed ticket out of a negative headspace. You don't have to donate a ton of money or volunteer in a soup kitchen to activate the positive energy flow of altruism; there's plenty of research that shows that *any* form of giving and being kind to others has a major impact on our health, longevity, happiness, and overall well-being. Since you're already invested in empowering Team Brave, how about aiming your efforts in the direction of a fellow woman? Might as well boost the sisterhood while you're getting yourself back on track! Offer your assistance to a colleague who is working on a big project. Reach out to a new mom in your kid's school and invite her for coffee. Send a personal note of thanks to a friend who supported or inspired you in some way. Visit the elderly woman who lives alone next door. Like gratitude, generosity pretty much vaporizes any lingering feelings of bitterness, shame, or disappointment and lifts you up, while at the same time bringing light and joy to someone else—so really, it's a win–win for everyone. When we realign with our generosity of spirit, we realign with our sense of purpose and bravery and can get back on track with what we want to do or accomplish.

Step Five: Try Again

You will falter. You will fuck up. You will have setbacks, flops, and failures. And yet . . .

Each time you screw up, you learn what not to do.

Each time you falter, you prove that you can right yourself.

Each time you fail, you get to try again.

Ultimately, your failures give you your edge. They make you stronger, wiser, more empathetic, more valuable, more real. And when you stop demanding perfection of yourself, they become your personal bravery badges of honor. Wear them with pride, and then get back out there and do it all over again.

I want every single one of us who have lived at the mercy of our perfect-girl training to know that no failure will break you. Will you make mistakes, maybe even fail? Absolutely. Will it break you? No way, sister. No mistake or setback will take you down once you become a die-hard member of Team Brave. Every setback is just another chance to further strengthen those fierce bravery muscles you're building by getting back up and trying again.

We are all in this together, and I believe with every fiber of my being that by practicing bravery every chance we get, we can create a powerful movement of strong, happy, fulfilled, and formidable women who can and will change the world.

So kiss that perfect girl goodbye and go be brave. It's your power to claim.

Acknowledgments

This book is a result of a lot of support from so many people in my sisterhood who inspire me on a daily basis. It started with the girls at Girls Who Code who inspired my TED talk and continued on with the many women who bravely shared their deepest fears and dreams with me.

I want to thank my writing partner Debra Goldstein. One of the best parts of writing this book was taking this journey with you. As a writer, it's a joy to find someone you can collaborate with—someone who pushes you to go deeper. I found that in Debra. Thank you for encouraging me to find my truth.

Thank you to Richard Pine, my incredible agent. You pushed me to write this book and have believed in this movement from the moment you saw me deliver that TED talk on stage. Thanks to Eliza Rothstein and the amazing team at Inkwell. I am happy to call you family!

Thank you to Tina Constable and the incredible team at Crown. To Candice from my publishing team, who made *Brave, Not Perfect* a permanent part of her life with a bnp tattoo, thank you for living this book every day. To my editor Talia Krohn, your brilliant editing and sage advice made this book come to life.

Thank you to Charlotte Stone for taking on this book and helping me create a bravery movement. You have put your heart and soul into elevating leadership for women and girls since you graduated college and I am grateful you took this journey with me.

Thank you, Priya Fielding-Singh, for your research and brilliant analytical mind. I am so grateful for the time and care you showed this book. Thank you, Sarah Beckoff, for your contribution and your support on this book.

Thank you to all the brilliant thinkers, authors, and change-makers who contributed their valuable insights and stories to this book: Dr. Catherine Steiner-Adair, Rachel Simmons, Dr. Andrew Shatte, Dr. Meredith Grossman, Adam Grant, Rha Goddess, Veronica Roth, Tiffany Dufu, Esther Perel, Bridget Moynahan, Danielle Weisberg, and Carly Zakin.

Thank you, Debbie Hanney, and Brad Brockmueller, for contributing your invaluable perspective as educators to this book.

Thanks to all the women and girls who participated in our brave not perfect focus groups and shared their stories with us. Writing this book taught me the obvious—that a mix of wine, sushi, and pizza can inspire honest sharing and lots of laughs.

Thank you to my Girls Who Code family and friends: Deborah Singer, Ben Yarrow, Trina Dasgupta, Rha Goddess, Tania Zaparaniuk, Ashley Gramby, and Emily Schienvar.

To the male allies in my life: my husband Nihal, my son Shaan, and my dad, thank you for inspiring me to always show up as my bravest self. And to my sister Keshma, my niece Maya, and my mom, thank you for teaching me so many life lessons.

Notes

Chapter One: Sugar and Spice and Everything Nice

19 **ascribe certain expectations** Sharon Begley, "Why Parents May Cause Gender Differences in Kids," *Newsweek*, September 2, 2009, http://www.newsweek.com/why-parents-may -cause-gender-differences-kids-79501

31 **women who earn B's** Claire Gorden, "Why Women Are Afraid of Failure," *Elle*, June 6, 2016, https://www.elle.com/ life-love/a36828/why-women-are-afraid-of-failure/

36 **Mansplaining and dominance** Eddie Wrenn, "The Great Gender Debate: Men Will Dominate 75% of the Conversation During Conference Meetings, Study Suggests," Daily Mail.com, September 12, 2012, http://www.dailymail.co.uk/sciencetech/ article-2205502/The-great-gender-debate-Men-dominate -75-conversation-conference-meetings-study-suggests.html

37 **We undervalue our contribution** Michelle C. Haynes and Madeline E. Heilman, "It Had to Be You (Not Me)! Women's Attributional Rationalization of Their Contribution to Successful Joint Work Outcomes," *Personality and Psychology Bulletin*, May 7, 2013, http://journals.sagepub.com/ doi/full/10.1177/0146167213486358

Chapter Two: The Cult of Perfection

44 **the gender marketing of toys** Elizabeth Sweet, "Toys Are More Divided by Gender Now Than They Were 50 Years Ago," *The Atlantic*, December 9, 2014, https://www.theatlan tic.com/business/archive/2014/12/toys-are-more-divided-by -gender-now-than-they-were-50-years-ago/383556/

44   **Professor Sarah M. Coyne observed** Sarah M. Coyne, et al., "Pretty as a Princess: Longitudinal Effects of Engagement with Disney Princesses on Gender Stereotypes, Body Esteem, and Prosocial Behavior in Children," *Child Development*, June 18, 2016, https://onlinelibrary.wiley.com/doi/abs/10.1111/cdev.12569

47   **twice as likely to take leading roles** Donna Ferguson, "Must Monsters Always Be Male? Huge Gender Bias Revealed in Children's Books," *The Guardian*, January 20, 2018, https://www.theguardian.com/books/2018/jan/21/childrens-books-sexism-monster-in-your-kids-book-is-male

Chapter Three: Perfection 3.0: When the Perfect Girl Grows Up

62   **On average, a woman spends 127 hours** Martha De Lacey, "Women spend ALMOST A YEAR counting calories and worrying about their weight during lifetime . . . but men aren't far behind!," Daily Mail.com, June 26, 2013, http://www.dailymail.co.uk/femail/article-2348972/Women-spend-year-counting-calories-worrying-weight-lifetime—men-arent-far-behind.html

62   **National Eating Disorders Association reports** UNC School of Medicine, "Statistics," accessed May 31, 2018, https://www.med.unc.edu/psych/eatingdisorders/Learn%20More/about-eating-disorders/statistics

66   **A seminal study done** Ross Douthat, "Liberated and Unhappy," May 25, 2009, https://www.nytimes.com/2009/05/26/opinion/26douthat.html

71   **A national survey** Kelly Sakai, "Work Is Not to Blame for Women's Lack of Free Time; Time-pressure Is Often Self-imposed, According to Real Simple/Families and Work Institute Survey," January 11, 2014, http://www.familiesandwork.org/the-results-of-a-new-groundbreaking-national-survey-women-and-time-setting-a-new-agenda-commissioned-by-real-simple-and-designed-by-families-and-work-institute-released/

75 **psychologist Thomas Greenspan** Melissa Dahl, "The Alarming New Research on Perfectionism," September 30, 2014, https://www.thecut.com/2014/09/alarming-new-research-on-perfectionism.html

78 **A study released in** McKinsey & Company, "Women in the Workplace," September 2015, https://www.mckinsey.com/business-functions/organization/our-insights/women-in-the-workplace

80 **Jennifer Lawrence discovered** Jennifer Lawrence, "Jennifer Lawrence: 'Why Do I Make Less Than My Male Co-Stars?'" October 13, 2015, https://www.lennyletter.com/story/jennifer-lawrence-why-do-i-make-less-than-my-male-costars

Chapter Four: Redefining Bravery

99 **the Crowdfunding Center** PWC, "Women Outperform Men in Seed Crowdfunding, According to Analysis by PwC and The Crowdfunding Centre," July 11, 2017, https://press.pwc.com/News-releases/women-outperform-men-in-seed-crowdfunding—according-to-analysis-by-pwc-and-the-crowdfunding-centre/s/ad6ee60a-c3be-478b-9e51-9a7ac4692cd3

Chapter Six: Build a Bravery Mindset

117 **It's not just that fatigue** Rand Corporation, "Lack of Sleep Costing U.S. Economy Up to $411 Billion a Year," November 30, 2016, https://www.rand.org/news/press/2016/11/30.html

119 **seven to nine hours a night** Ibid.

120 **the "power of yet"** Carol Dweck, "The Power of Believing That You Can Improve," TED Talk, November 2014, https://www.ted.com/talks/carol_dweck_the_power_of_believing_that_you_can_improve

126 **Alice Paul Tapper noticed** Alice Paul Tapper, "I'm 10, and I Want Girls to Raise Their Hands," *New York Times*, October 31, 2017, https://www.nytimes.com/2017/10/31/opinion/im-10-and-i-want-girls-to-raise-their-hands.html?_r=0

Chapter Seven: Get Caught Trying

136 **Cecile Richards, the formidable former president of Planned Parenthood** Dayna Evans, "Cecile Richards: If You're Not Pissing People Off, You're Probably Not Doing Your Job," *The Cut,* July 19, 2017, https://www.thecut.com/2017/07/cecile-richards-planned-parenthood-interview-92y.html

140 **famous study of London cabdrivers** Eleanor A. Maguire, Katherine Woollett, and Hugo J. Spiers, "London Taxi Drivers and Bus Drivers: A Structural MRI and Neuropsychological Analysis," *Hippocampus*, October 5, 2006, https://www.psychologytoday.com/files/u81/Maguire__Woollett__and_Spiers__2006_.pdf

140 **research has shown that gray matter increases** David Marchese, et al., "Why You Suck at Stuff and How to Get Better," *The Cut,* November 17, 2016, http://nymag.com/scienceofus/2016/11/why-you-suck-at-stuff-and-how-to-get-better.html

Chapter Eight: Nix the Need to Please

150 **Helen Mirren** Michelle Lee, "Why Helen Mirren Wishes She'd Said 'Fuck Off' More as a Young Woman," *Allure*, August 14, 2017, https://www.allure.com/story/helen-mirren-cover-story-september-2017

156 **see themselves as far more assertive than others do** Daniel Ames and Abbie Wazlewek, "Pushing in the Dark: Causes and Consequences of Limited Self-Awareness for Interpersonal Assertiveness," *Personality and Social Psychology Bulletin*, February 28, 2014, http://www.columbia.edu/~da358/publications/Pushing_in_the_dark.pdf

157 **being interrupted, talked over, shut down** Susan Chira, "The Universal Phenomenon of Men Interrupting Women," *New York Times*, June 14, 2017, https://www.nytimes.com/2017/06/14/business/women-sexism-work-huffington-kamala-harris.html?_r=0

158 **Chelsea Manning faced an onslaught of pressure** Jennifer McDermott, "Chelsea Manning: 'I Believe I Did the Best I

Could,'" *Daily Herald*, September 17, 2017, http://www.daily
herald.com/article/20170917/news/309179906

159   **discredit Taylor Swift** Christopher Rosa, "Taylor Swift's
10 Most Powerful Statements from Her Sexual Assault Trial
Cross-Examination," *Glamour*, August 10, 2017, https://www
.glamour.com/story/taylor-swift-sexual-assault-trial-cross
-examination?mbid=social_facebook_fanpage

Chapter Nine: Play for Team Brave

165   **very real obstacles to gender equality** Olga Kahzan, "Why
Do Women Bully Each Other at Work?," *The Atlantic*, September 2017, https://www.theatlantic.com/magazine/archive
/2017/09/the-queen-bee-in-the-corner-office/534213/

Chapter Ten: Surviving a Big, Fat Failure

171   **In 2013, the outlook was promising** Damian Garde, "How
to Fail Well in Biotech: Shed a Tear, Grab a Trophy, and
Move On," STAT, August 17, 2016, https://www.statnews
.com/2016/08/17/biotech-drug-development-failure/

172   **When I say, "shake it off,"** Brian Iacoviello and Dennis
Charney, "Psychosocial Facets of Resilience: Implications for
Preventing Posttrauma Psychopathology, Treating Trauma
Survivors, and Enhancing Community Resilience," *European
Journal of Psychotraumatology*, October 1, 2014, https://www
.ncbi.nlm.nih.gov/pmc/articles/PMC4185137/

175   **Elizabeth Gilbert shares how** Elizabeth Gilbert, "Success,
Failure, and the Drive to Keep Creating," TED talk, March
2014, https://www.ted.com/talks/elizabeth_gilbert_success
_failure_and_the_drive_to_keep_creating#t-415147

175   **Gratitude is a potent and proven** J. Vieselmeyer, J. Hol-
guin, and A. Mezulis, "The Role of Resilience and Gratitude in Posttraumatic Stress and Growth Following a Campus
Shooting," January 9, 2017, https://www.ncbi.nlm.nih.gov/
pubmed/27548470

175   **Oprah Winfrey fell into a depression** Jonathan Van Meter,
"Oprah Is on a Roll (Again)," *Vogue*, August 15, 2017, https://

www.vogue.com/article/oprah-winfrey-vogue-september
-issue-2017

176　**altruism is a guaranteed ticket** Stephen G. Post, "Altruism,
Happiness, and Health: It's Good to Be Good," *International
Journal of Behavioral Medicine*, 2005, https://greatergood.berkeley
.edu/images/uploads/Post-AltruismHappinessHealth.pdf

176　**generosity pretty much vaporizes** Alex Dixon, "Kindness Makes You Happy . . . and Happiness Makes You Kind,"
Greater Good Magazine, September 6, 2011, https://greatergood
.berkeley.edu/article/item/kindness_makes_you_happy_and
_happiness_makes_you_kind

Index

people pleasing
  being in own truth and,
    147–148
  as part of pursuit of perfection,
    6, 22
  toxicity of, 23–24
Perel, Esther, 96, 103, 173–174
perfectionism. *See also* myths of
    perfection
  agreeing to all requests and,
    154
  as complex knot of lifelong
    beliefs, expectations, and
    fears, 59–60
  as endless cycle, 29–30
  fear of not achieving, holds
    women back, 78–82
  female body and, 61–65
  happiness and, 7, 65–67
  as illusion, 162–164
  impedes bravery, 97
  impedes excellence, 73–75
  impedes risk-taking, 6, 76
  impossibility of, 74
  is boring, 82–83
  as lesson taught to girls, 4–5
  mistakes and, 134
  motherhood and, 70–71,
    95–96
  overpreparation and, 6, 30,
    121–122
  people pleasing as part of,
    6, 22
  "personal branding," 49
  pressures increase with age, 17
  pride in, 30–31
  sleep and, 6, 118–119
  wage gap and, 80
"personal branding," 49

physical activity, 172
pity parties, 170
play, effects of gender cultural
    indoctrination on, 43–45
"playing it safe," as part of girls'
    upbringing, 4–5
power of "yet," 119–121
"princess culture," 44
priorities and saying "no,"
    154–155
"process praise," 34
procrastination and risk-taking,
    123–124, 135–137
protection
  ability to fail and, 28–29
  as necessary for girls, 26, 27

"reframing your narrative,"
    173–174
rejection, exposure to, 132–133
resilience
  building, by normalizing
    failure and mistakes, 132
  as characteristic of boys, 26
  physical activity and, 172
Rhimes, Shonda, 98
Richards, Cecile, 136, 137
"right" answers, calculation of,
    21–22
Rihanna, 64
risk-taking
  attempting new physical
    challenges, 141–143
  attempting previous failures,
    139–140
  children's lessons about, 4–5
  doing "male" tasks, 143–145
  failure as increasing chances
    for success, 177

Discussion Questions

1. Which part of *Brave, Not Perfect* resonated the most with you? Did you recognize yourself in any of the stories?

2. Do you ever feel like you are putting too much pressure on yourself to be perfect? To win gold stars at work? To "do it all" as a mom? To be nice and polite, at all times? Do you think this pressure is holding you back in any area of your life?

3. Do you ever feel like you're living the life others expect from you rather than the one you authentically want? If you could change anything without worrying about "letting someone down," what would it be?

4. In the opening chapter, Reshma talks about how running for Congress was the first time she did anything that she wasn't positive she could succeed at. Have you ever shied away from challenges or opportunities because you feared you would fail, look silly, or that it would take you outside your comfort zone?

5. Do you ever worry about seeming too aggressive, or about "not being liked," at work? Do you think the men in your position feel the same way? How can you tell?

6. Reshma writes about how "today, social media feeds the expectation of polished perfection perhaps more than any other influence out there." Does looking at photos of

people's "perfect" family or "perfect" vacation or "perfect" lives on social media make you feel inadequate? Do you refuse to post something that's any less polished for fear of what others might think? If you have a daughter, is she experiencing social media the same way?

7. In the book, Reshma talks about how as women we tend to treat our appearance as our armor. Do you ever think that if you look polished and flawless—thin, full face of makeup, not a hair out of place—people can't judge you? That you'll somehow be "safe"?

8. One of the myths debunked in the book is this idea of "perfection is the same as excellence." Even when we know that we can be excellent without being perfect, it's often hard to find the line. Where is that line for you?

9. If you are a parent of both boys and girls, do you notice any ways in which you might inadvertently be treating them differently when it comes to perfection and bravery?

10. If you have girls, what are some ways you might model bravery for your daughter(s)? How can you teach her that it's okay to fail?

11. Count how many times you apologize in one day. Can you try going one day without making a single apology and see how that feels?

12. Have you ever gotten stuck in a cycle of rumination, worrying that you offended someone, or said the wrong thing? What would be the worst that could happen, even if you did?

13. In chapter six, Reshma talks about the idea of finding our "ledge," the one thing that scares us the most. What is your

"ledge"? And how would your life improve if you faced that fear?

14. Part two of the book is full of stories of courageous women of all ages who are changing the world, one brave act at a time. We all need more (realistic) brave role models like these. Who is yours?

15. In chapter seven, Reshma explains how "getting caught trying" helps us build a resilience to failure. What's one thing you can try—and maybe fail at—today?

16. At the very end of the book, Reshma talks about the importance of sisterhood—or what she calls "playing for team brave." What's one thing you can do tomorrow to support another woman's bravery?

17. How else will you use the insights and tools in this book to jump-start your brave, not perfect life?

Want to
Jump-start Your

*Brave,
Not
Perfect*

life?

Take the
Brave, Not Perfect
Challenge

visit reshmasaujani.com